UEFA

EURO 2016
FRANCE

THE OFFICIAL BOOK

First published in 2016

Manufactured under licence by Carlton Books Ltd
An imprint of the Carlton Publishing Group
20 Mortimer Street, London W1T 3JW

Editorial Director: Martin Corteel
Design Manager: Luke Griffin
Design: Rockjaw Creative
Picture Research: Paul Langan
Production: Maria Petalidou

10 9 8 7 6 5 4 3 2 1

A catalogue record for this book is available
from the British Library.

ISBN 978-1-78097-757-7

Printed in Slovenia

RIGHT: Launched at EURO 2008, the updated
version of the Henri Delaunay Cup is based
on the original design but is on a grander
scale and features an enlarged base for added
stability and has the names of the winning
teams engraved on the back of the trophy
instead of appearing on the plinth.

UEFA
EURO2016
FRANCE

THE OFFICIAL BOOK

Keir Radnedge

CARLTON
BOOKS

The Stade de France, in Saint-Denis, on the outskirts of Paris, with a capacity of 80,000, is home to the national team. It has hosted many major sporting and entertainment events, including both FIFA World Cup and Rugby World Cup finals.

CONTENTS

BELOW: **Star Men (from left):** Gareth Bale, Eden Hazard, Wayne Rooney, Andres Iniesta, Robert Lewandowski, Cristiano Ronaldo and Manuel Neuer.

INTRODUCTION

The finals of UEFA EURO 2016 are just around the corner, a further exciting step for European national team football and a competition that magnetises the attention of fans around the world.

Host France is a country steeped in football's great traditions and great deeds. The national team have won the UEFA European Football Championship twice – in 1984 as hosts and in 2000 – as well as the FIFA World Cup. Off the pitch, Frenchmen played leading roles in building the organisations and competitions that thrill European supporters from Valencia to Vladivostok.

That tradition has been evident at every step of the way. Frenchman Henri Delaunay had the dream of a European championship and provided much of the momentum that saw the creation of the European federation, UEFA, in the mid-1950s.

France played host to the inaugural finals in 1960, when the Soviet Union defeated Yugoslavia in the final in the old Parc des Princes. Some 24 years later, when the tournament returned to France, a superb host team inspired by captain and then leading scorer Michel Platini defeated Spain 2–0 in the final in the rebuilt Parc des Princes.

Sixteen years later, France were winning again in neighbouring Belgium and the Netherlands with a team led by the likes of Zinedine Zidane and Didier Deschamps – who duly became national coach four years ago.

The growth of the UEFA European Football Championship is a reflection of its increasing popularity and the will of every European footballer to step out onto the continent's grandest stage.

Initially, the finals were contested between four teams, in two semi-finals, a third-place play-off and the final. In 1980, UEFA decided that more countries should be welcomed to the party and doubled the complement to eight teams. Sixteen years later, in 1996, England became the first host to boast a 16-team tournament.

The hallmark of the UEFA European Football Championship has been magnificent and dramatic football, so it was no wonder that more national associations wanted to share in the four-yearly festival. Hence the decision taken by UEFA, under the presidency of Platini, to expand the finals by an extra eight nations.

France will, therefore, be the first nation to stage a 24-team tournament in the ten magnificent venues that will be opening their gates to a flood of home and international supporters from 10 June to 10 July.

The 268 matches of the qualifying competition produced 694 goals with Poland's Robert Lewandowski the 13-goal leading marksman, but now it's all back to square one. Everyone starts from zero ... with everything to play for.

LEFT: A spectacular can-can kick-off to the finals draw in Paris's Palais des Congrès last December.

OPPOSITE: All Europe's leading nations were represented in sound, dance and colour on stage in Paris.

Chapter 1
Welcome to France

FRANCE, IN HOSTING UEFA EURO 2016, WILL BECOME THE FIRST NATION TO STAGE THE FINALS THREE TIMES, AFTER 1960 AND 1984. TWO NATIONS HAVE PLAYED HOST ON TWO OCCASIONS: ITALY IN 1968 AND 1980 THEN BELGIUM IN 1972 AND AS CO-HOSTS IN 2000. THE ITALIANS, IN 1968, ARE ONE OF ONLY THREE NATIONS TO HAVE CAPITALISED ON HOME ADVANTAGE TO WIN THE ULTIMATE PRIZE, ALONG WITH SPAIN IN 1964 AND *LES BLEUS* IN 1984. FRANCE CAN NOW MAKE IT TWO OUT OF THREE.

The Henri Delaunay Trophy is coming back home to France. The UEFA European Football Championship was the brainchild of former UEFA General Secretary Henri Delaunay and France, his home country, is the first nation to be host to the finals on three occasions. The last two occasions France hosted major football championships – EURO 84 and 1998 FIFA World Cup – *Les Bleus* were the tournament winners.

BACKGROUND AND PREPARATIONS

European football thoughts first focused on EURO UEFA 2016 was back on 28 May 2010. That was when the European governing body's executive committee voted to decide the host of the first tournament to feature an expanded 24-team field.

An expansion from 16 to 24 nations had been debated widely throughout the European game. The FIFA World Cup had shown how steady expansion had benefitted football's development across the length, breadth and depth of the continental game. UEFA Congress decided to follow suit, approving the concept in 2009.

The expansion invited excited speculation about an escalation of the competitive nature of the qualifying tournament. UEFA maintained its standard groups system and also introduced a centralised sale of television rights based around a "Week of Football" concept.

This meant that European national team football could be broadcast worldwide regularly over five successive days every month of the mainstream fixture schedule. In short, it created a European football showcase.

UEFA formally launched the bidding process on 11 December 2008. Initially it set a minimum demand of nine all-seater stadia with three in reserve. Later, after it was confirmed that the tournament had been expanded to 24 teams, UEFA increased their demand of "active" stadia number to ten or 11.

When it came to decision time France, Italy and Turkey were the contenders after bids from other initially interested national associations did not materialise.

Turkey was bidding to land the finals for the first time. It had campaigned previously, albeit in vain, to co-host the 2008 finals together with Greece. On this occasion the Turkish federation had presented an ambitious project that would require eight new stadia. In contrast, Italy proposed no new stadia but promised to upgrade 12 established venues.

France balanced its bid between these two extremes. The French federation had declared its intention to bid, with government encouragement, well before the formal launch.

It proposed four new venues – in Lyon, Lille, Bordeaux and Nice – plus the redevelopment of eight. In the end, ten stadia were confirmed, with the new venue in Lyon, costing €405m, the last to be completed. The Stade de France in Saint-Denis, north of Paris, was a natural choice for the final. The 81,338-capacity national stadium had hosted the finals of both the 1998 FIFA World Cup and 2007 Rugby World Cup.

On 28 May 2010, two rounds of balloting were needed. First time round, UEFA's executive committee members voted on a points basis. France gained 43, Turkey 38 and Italy was eliminated with 23. The second round of voting was through simple preference. France edged Turkey by one vote: 7–6.

France has twice hosted the finals. The inaugural 1960 final (between the Soviet Union and Yugoslavia) was staged in the old Parc des Princes while

LEFT: The French delegation, with Zinedine Zidane, left centre, and other former players and officials, celebrate the May 2010 announcement that they would host EURO 2016.

ABOVE: Super Victor, the mascot for UEFA EURO 2016, says, "I love to bring people together to play football!"

the 1984 showdown (between France and Spain) was hosted in the successor venue on an adjacent site.

Those very first finals, in 1960, featured four teams, who played knockout semi-finals, the final and a third-place match. That formula continued until 1980, when the field was increased to eight teams, split into two groups of four, with the winners of each group going directly to the final. From 1984, the top two teams in each group contested knockout semi-finals.

The number of finalists was increased to 16 for UEFA EURO 1996. The teams were divided into four groups of four, with knockout quarter-finals, semi-finals and a final. This pattern continued until the tournament was staged in Poland and Ukraine four years ago.

Expanding the number of teams in the tournament means an extra two groups and an extra round in the knockout stages. Therefore, UEFA EURO 2016 will feature 51 matches instead of 31.

Building work on the stadia started almost immediately. The total cost of stadia work has been estimated at €1.6bn generated from a mixture of private and public-private funding projects. Supervising preparations has been a steering committee that has been meeting regularly since 2011. Represented on the committee are all the major stakeholders: UEFA, the French federation, the French government and the host cities. The chairman of the committee is Jacques Lambert who gained vast personal experience when he performed a similar role when France hosted the FIFA World Cup 18 years ago.

No major football event is complete without its official mascot and song and UEFA EURO 2016 is no exception. The mascot was introduced in November 2014. The representation was styled as "half child, half superhero ... a curious, witty character who will encourage fans from all over the world to celebrate the 'art of football'". The mascot Super Victor won with 48 per cent of the public vote, ahead of Goalix (27 per cent) and Driblou (25 per cent).

The official song was commissioned to be written and produced by French DJ and music producer David Guetta, who will also perform it at the opening ceremony in the Stade de France. According to UEFA, Guetta was handed a wider remit: he has been asked to create "the musical identity for the entire tournament: everything from in-stadia audio to global broadcast sequences". He will also stage a free concert at the Champ de Mars in the shadow of the Eiffel Tower on the eve of the tournament.

The tournament is set to attract a record number of football tourists to France, perhaps as many as 10 million – justifying the welcoming official slogan of *Le Rendez-Vous*. Between 10 June and 10 July 2016, France looks set to become a magnetic meeting point for all of European football.

THE VENUES

France has a grand tradition for big occasions. Every one of the selected venues has hosted dramatic and historic matches in either or both the FIFA World Cup and the UEFA European Football Championship, as well as the European club competitions.

SAINT-DENIS
STADE DE FRANCE

The French national stadium was built for the 1998 FIFA World Cup and is the only venue to have staged the final match of both the FIFA World Cup and the Rugby World Cup. It was also the venue for two UEFA Champions League finals: Real Madrid CF's 3–0 win against Valencia CF in 2000 and FC Barcelona's 2–1 triumph over Arsenal FC six years later. Retractable seating also permits athletics competition. Three U2 concerts in 2009 and 2010 attracted a total of 283,084 fans.

Capacity: 80,000
Matches hosted:
Group A – France v Romania (10 June)
Group E – Rep Ireland v Sweden (13 June)
Group C – Germany v Poland (16 June)
Group F – Iceland v Austria (22 June)
Round of 16 (43) – WE v RD (27 June)
Quarter-final (48) – W40 v W44 (3 July)
Final EURO 2016 – W49 v W50 (10 July)

MARSEILLE
STADE VÉLODROME

After a €267 million redevelopment, which was completed in September 2014, this famous venue now includes a roof. The Stade Vélodrome boasted a cycling track on its original opening in 1937, which was marked by a match between Marseille and Italy's Torino. It staged matches at the 1938 and 1998 FIFA World Cups as well as the 1960 and 1984 UEFA European Football Championships. It has also hosted athletics, rugby, boxing, tennis and hockey, as well as concerts and political rallies.

Capacity: 67,000
Matches hosted:
Group B – England v Russia (11 June)
Group A – France v Albania (15 June)
Group F – Iceland v Hungary (18 June)
Group C – Ukraine v Poland (21 June)
Quarter-final (45) – W37 v W39 (30 June)
Semi-final (50) – W47 v W48 (7 July)

LYON
STADE DE LYON

The Stade de Lyon has taken over as the focus of sport in Lyon, replacing the Stade de Gerland which was Olympique Lyonnais's home since 1950 and one of seven venues for the 1984 UEFA European Football Championship, hosting Denmark's 5–0 group-stage win over Yugoslavia and the Denmark v Spain semi-final. It was also a FIFA World Cup venue in 1998. Olympique Lyonnais's club president Jean-Michel Aulas laid the foundation stone for the new stadium in November 2013, and its official inauguration was in January 2016.

Capacity: 59,000
Matches hosted:
Group E – Belgium v Italy (13 June)
Group C – Ukraine v N Ireland (16 June)
Group A – Romania v Albania (19 June)
Group F – Hungary v Portugal (22 June)
Round of 16 (40) – WA v 3C/D/E (26 June)
Semi-final (49) – W45 v W46 (6 July)

BELOW: The Stade Vélodrome in Marseille may be almost 80 years old, and hosted matches in two FIFA World Cups and two UEFA European Football Championships, but its has undergone an amazing facelift for UEFA EURO 2016 and now boasts a futuristic roof.

LILLE MÉTROPOLE
STADE PIERRE MAUROY

Opened in 2012, the multi-purpose stadium has more than twice the capacity of local club LOSC's old home, Stade Grimonprez-Jooris, and Stadium Lille Métropole. AS Nancy-Lorraine's Djamel Bakar scored the venue's first goal in August 2012 – Salomon Kalou equalised for LOSC. The venue's first international sporting action came in November 2012, when France's rugby union side beat Argentina 39–22, and it has since hosted major basketball and tennis events.

Capacity: 50,000
Matches hosted:
Group C – Germany v Ukraine (12 June)
Group B – Russia v Slovakia (15 June)
Group A – Switzerland v France (19 June)
Group E – Italy v Rep Ireland (22 June)
Round of 16 (41) – WC v 3A/B/F (26 June)
Quarter-final (46) – W38 v W42 (1 July)

PARIS
PARC DES PRINCES

The old Parc des Princes provided the finish line of the Tour de France from 1903 and 1967, hosted matches at the 1938 FIFA World Cup and staged the finals of the first European Champion Clubs' Cup in 1956 and the UEFA European Football Championship in 1960. It was then razed and rebuilt in the mid-1970s, hosting the final matches again of the European Football Championship and the Champions Cup as well as matches at the 1998 FIFA World Cup.

Capacity: 48,000
Matches hosted:
Group D – Turkey v Croatia (12 June)
Group A – Romania v Switzerland (15 June)
Group F – Portugal v Austria (18 June)
Group C – N Ireland v Germany (21 June)
Round of 16 (38) – WB v 3A/C/D (25 June)

SAINT-ÉTIENNE
STADE GEOFFROY-GUICHARD

Home to AS Saint-Étienne, 10 times French champions, Stade Geoffroy-Guichard is an "English-style" stadium, with its distinctive four separate stands. The original venue incorporated an athletics track that was removed in 1956 ahead of an initial redevelopment. It staged matches at the 1984 UEFA European Football Championship, the 1998 FIFA World Cup and the 2007 Rugby World Cup. It is nicknamed *Le Chaudron* (The Cauldron) for its passionate, big-match atmosphere.

Capacity: 42,000
Matches hosted:
Group F – Portugal v Iceland (14 June)
Group D – Czech Rep v Croatia (17 June)
Group B – Slovakia v England (20 June)
Round of 16 (37) – RA v RC (25 June)

BORDEAUX
STADE DE BORDEAUX

Bordeaux football's new home cost €184 million and took a little more than two years to build from the start of construction in 2013. City mayor Alain Juppé described the design as "a piece of art which will enrich our cultural heritage" on its opening in May 2015. The multifunctional venue is the new home of Girondins de Bordeaux whose original Stade Chaban-Delmas home staged matches at the 1938 and 1998 FIFA World Cups.

Capacity: 42,000
Matches hosted:
Group B – Wales v Slovakia (11 June)
Group F – Austria v Hungary (14 June)
Group E – Belgium v Rep Ireland (18 June)
Group D – Croatia v Spain (21 June)
Quarter-final (47) – W41 v W43 (2 July)

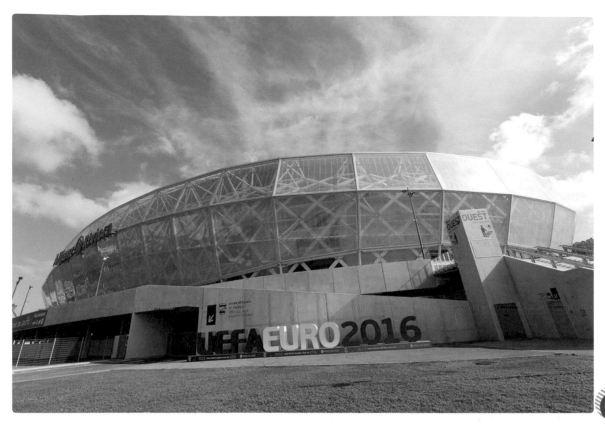

ABOVE: Nice is the largest city on the French Riviera, and now it has a football stadium to match its beautiful location. Located 10km from the city centre and 5km from the airport, it is close to the A8 motorway so access to the 35,000-capacity venue will be easy.

OPPOSITE: The new stadium in Bordeaux features white seats, similar to the Stade Chaban-Delmas, but it is a significantly better and more modern arena with sightlines that give all spectators a superb view of the action and they are still very close to the action.

NICE
STADE DE NICE

Designed by Jean-Michel Wilmotte , the Stade de Nice is the stunning new home for OGC Nice. Work began on the stadium in 2011 and it saw its first action in September 2013 when OGC Nice defeated Valenciennes FC 4–0. France's sixth largest football stadium also houses the *Musée National du Sport* (National Sport Museum), which moved from Paris and was officially opened on 15 October 2014. More than 45,000 items and 400,000 documents are on show there.

Capacity: 36,000
Matches hosted:
Group C – Poland v N Ireland (12 June)
Group D – Spain v Turkey (17 June)
Group E – Sweden v Belgium (22 June)
Round of 16 (44)– RB v RF (27 June)

LENS AGGLO
STADE BOLLAERT-DELELIS

Now 83 years old, the stadium was built in the early 1930s by unemployed miners and was named after the former commercial director of the Lens Mining Company, Félix Bollaert. Later, in September 2012, its name evolved in tribute to Lens' former city mayor and long-time fan, André Delelis. It staged matches at the 1984 UEFA European Football Championship, the 1998 FIFA World Cup and was a venue at the 2007 Rugby World Cup. Since then, the stadium has undergone major renovations.

Capacity: 38,000
Matches hosted:
Group A – Albania v Switzerland (11 June)
Group B – England v Wales (16 June)
Group D – Czech Rep v Turkey (21 June)
Round of 16 (39) – WD v 38B/E/F (25 June)

TOULOUSE
STADIUM DE TOULOUSE

Situated on an island in the heart of Toulouse, the stadium was built specifically for the 1938 FIFA World Cup and was nicknamed "mini Wembley" after its resemblance to the original old design of the London venue. Significant renovations were made to the stadium in 1949, 1997 – it staged six matches during the 1998 FIFA World Cup – and again in 2015. The stadium was another of the UEFA EURO 2016 venues to have hosted matches in the 2007 Rugby World Cup.

Capacity: 33,000
Matches hosted:
Group D – Spain v Czech Rep (13 June)
Group E – Italy v Sweden (17 June)
Group B – Russia v Wales (20 June)
Round of 16 (42) – WF v RE (26 June)

FRENCH FOOTBALL HEROES

French football has played a key role in building the international football monolith. Frenchmen played a crucial role in creating the European and world governing bodies, the FIFA World Cup, the UEFA European Football Championship and the European Champion Clubs' Cup, which evolved into today's UEFA Champions League.

Long-serving FIFA president Jules Rimet was the driving force behind the launch of its World Cup in 1930 and fellow countryman and first UEFA General Secretary Henri Delaunay's dream turned into reality when the first the UEFA European Football Championship was staged in 1960.

Paris hosted the first European Champion Clubs' Cup final in 1956 and the climax of the inaugural UEFA European Football Championship (originally the European Nations' Cup) in 1960. On both occasions the venue was the original Parc des Princes, which was razed in the early 1970s to make way for the grand stadium that now bears the same name.

French footballers have also played their part in the game's history. Lucien Laurent struck the first goal in the inaugural FIFA World Cup and Reims reached the first European Champion Clubs' Cup final in 1956 and then again in 1959 (losing both to all-conquering CF Real Madrid). The Champagne region club also provided the nucleus of the national team who finished third at the 1958 FIFA World Cup.

In 1958, schemer Raymond Kopa, who had just won the European Champion Clubs' Cup with Madrid, became France's first European

RIGHT: Raymond Kopa, France's first superstar schemer, played in the 1954 and 1958 FIFA World Cup finals and in qualifying matches for the 1960 UEFA European Nations' Cup.

Footballer of the Year. He created the majority of the tournament-record 13 goals Just Fontaine, his centre-forward successor at Reims, scored at the 1958 FIFA World Cup.

The next great flowering of individual talent blossomed in the late 1970s. In 1976 France reached the quarter-finals of the Montreal Olympic Games, and they were unlucky to be knocked out in the group stages of the FIFA World Cup in Argentina two years later. Both teams drew their attacking inspiration from a goal-hungry youngster from Joeuf in Lorraine named Michel Platini. He was nurtured and encouraged by Michel Hidalgo, who had stepped up as national coach in 1976 and brought with him all the experience he had gained as right-winger with Reims and France in the late 1950s.

Hidalgo entrusted Platini with both the captaincy and, as a natural leader, a freedom of action across the attack. His career was marked by decisive steps up the ladder of fame and fortune: from Nancy-Lorraine to Saint-Etienne and then, in 1982, to Juventus.

For three successive seasons between 1982–83 and 1984–85, Platini finished as Serie A's leading scorer, and inspired the "Old Lady" to win the FIFA World Club Cup (in 1985), the European Champion Clubs' Cup (1985), the now-defunct UEFA Cup-Winners' Cup (1984) and UEFA Super Cup (1984). Along the way he was hailed as European Footballer of the Year on three occasions (in 1983, 1984 and 1985). A greater player than Kopa, he was eventually superseded in stature only by Zinedine Zidane.

Platini secured his status as leader of *Les Bleus* over a 72-game international career that brought him a then-record 41 goals. Two of them came as France reached the semi-finals of the 1982 FIFA World Cup. Defeat then, on penalties to West Germany, was bitter indeed, but the experience of pressure at the highest level proved invaluable two years later when France hosted the European finals.

By now Platini was not the only French football icon. Midfielders Alain

Giresse, the tireless Jean Tigana and powerful Luis Fernandez not only supported him but established their own international reputations.

Spain-born Fernandez provided the power to break down opposing attacks. Bordeaux's Giresse provided creative guile and a memorable goal in the dramatic 1982 FIFA World Cup semi-final against West Germany. Tigana, been born in Mali, had come to France with his family as a child. At 20, Toulon gave him away on a free transfer, only for future FIFA World Cup-winning coach Aimé Jacquet to "rescue" him for Lyon.

Along with Platini they comprised the "Magic Square", the trio providing crucial support for their captain's title-winning displays. His nine goals in five games included hat-tricks against Belgium and Yugoslavia, a last-minute extra-time winner in the semi-final against Portugal and the first goal in a 2–0 victory over Spain in the final.

Some 14 years later, and Platini was back in a key role – this time in the VIP box. After a stint as manager of France, between 1988 and 1992, he became joint president of the

organising committee for the 1998 FIFA World Cup.

It was during that tournament that France finally landed the prize that had eluded Kopa and Platini – and triumph came courtesy of the inspirational Zinedine Zidane.

"Zizou" wrote headlines from his teenage days with Bordeaux right through to the very end of his career. In between he had starred in Italy, with Juventus, and in Spain, for Real Madrid, with whom he won the UEFA Champions League in 2002. Most important for French football, however, was the decisive role he played in France's international double.

In 1998, Zidane scored two of the goals as France defeated Brazil 3–0 in the final to win the FIFA World Cup. Two years later, at UEFA EURO 2000 in Belgium and the Netherlands, he led *Les Bleus* to further success. Statistics reinforce his status. With 31 goals from midfield in 108 games Zidane stands fourth in the all-time French scoring and appearances lists.

A new Kopa, Platini or Zidane could just be about to explode to glory this time around.

ABOVE: When France hosted the 1984 UEFA European Football Championship, Michel Platini was at the peak of his career, and he inspired the team to glory in the final against Spain.

MOST APPEARANCES

1	Lilian Thuram	142
2	Thierry Henry	123
3	Marcel Desailly	116
4	Zinedine Zidane	108
5	Patrick Vieira	107
6	Didier Deschamps	103
7	Laurent Blanc	97
8	Bixente Lizarazu	97
9	Sylvain Wiltord	92
10	Fabian Barthez	87

TOP GOALSCORERS

1	Thierry Henry	51
2	Michel Platini	41
3	David Trezeguet	34
4	Zinedine Zidane	31
5	Just Fontaine	30
6	Jean-Pierre Papin	30
7	Youri Djorkaeff	28
8	Karim Benzema	27
9	Sylvain Wiltord	26
10	Jean Vincent	22

ABOVE: Zinedine Zidane was the central focus of France's greatest era, when *Les Bleus* won the 1998 FIFA World Cup and 2000 UEFA European Football Championship.

How appropriate it was that
Paris, the city with a landmark,
l'Arc de Triomphe (the Arch of
Triumph) should be a focal point
of the victory parade for France's
1998 FIFA World Cup winning
squad. Their victory in the
final, at the end of a gloriously
successful tournament, had come
just a few kilometres away, at the
Stade de France, in Saint-Denis.

THE DRAW

Can-Can dancers kicked off the show the evening the draw for the finals launched the six-month countdown to UEFA EURO 2016. The headline outcome for the French hosts was knowing they will take on Romania in the opening match in the Stade de France on 10 June.

Opening up the four-yearly tournament to 24 teams rather than 16 brought more national association delegates than ever to the Palais des Congrès in Paris. Gianni Infantino, UEFA's general secretary, presided over the draw with the assistance of old heroes such as Antonín Panenka, Oliver Bierhoff, David Trezeguet and Angelos Charisteas, with Ruud Gullit and Bixente Lizarazu as MCs.

France were the only team with a pre-designated slot in the draw, while the other 23 nations had been placed in four separate pots according to the UEFA coefficient rankings. The other five top seeds were drawn across the remaining five groups. Then came the pot containing the lowest-ranked nations, followed by Pot 3 and then Pot 2, with dangerous "floaters" such as Italy and Poland.

France coach Didier Deschamps was satisfied to learn that Les Bleus will follow up their opener against Romania on 10 June with further group ties against finals newcomers Albania in Marseille five days later and then south-east neighbours Switzerland in Lille on 19 June.

He said: "We don't know the Romanian team that well, even though they performed very well during the qualification stage with the best defence and just two goals against. It will be the most important match for us. We have to be careful and not over-confident."

England, top seeds in Group B, were drawn against familiar opposition in neighbours Wales, who will be contesting a first major tournament finals since the 1958 FIFA World Cup. Their meeting in Lens on 16 June will be the second outing for both sides. It will also be

the nations' 102nd meeting since they first clashed in 1879. England have won 66 times and Wales 14.

Russia and Slovakia completed Group B, with the Russians, like England, determined to make amends in France for their disappointing early elimination at the 2014 FIFA World Cup.

Germany, triumphant in Brazil, were top seeds in Group C, but have not won the European title since their third success back in 1996. Thomas Müller and Co open up against Ukraine in Lille on 12 June before facing Poland in the Stade de France

RIGHT: Old heroes Bixente Lizarazu, Ruud Gullit, Antonin Panenka, Oliver Bierhoff, David Trezeguet and Angelos Charisteas undertake the draw.

OPPOSITE: Facing up for Group B, from left: Stefan Tarkovic (Slovakia assistant coach), Roy Hodgson (England manager), Leonid Slutski (Russia coach and Chris Coleman (Wales coach).

and winding up against Northern Ireland in the Parc des Princes.

Coach Joachim Löw said: "Poland are a great side, but Ukraine and Northern Ireland can be difficult to play against too, with their counterattacks and strong defending. We are the favourites and want to win the group."

Champions Spain launch their defence in Group D against the Czech Republic in Toulouse on 13 June. They face Turkey and Croatia, who were among Spain's group stage opponents four years ago in Poland and Ukraine.

Spain coach Vicente del Bosque cautioned that the quality of both the Czechs and the Turks could be judged by their emergence from the qualifying group in which the Netherlands fell short. He also considered Croatia as "among the strongest teams at this tournament".

The European champions have sharp memories of the talents of Croatia. In 2012, Spain won only 1–0 with a goal two minutes from the end by Jesús Navas. Spain then went on to win the title again, so they may regard the repeat as a lucky omen.

Belgium, who went into 2016 as the top team in the world according to the FIFA rankings, found themselves with an awkward test in Group E along with Italy, Sweden and Ireland. For some observers this was the "group of death", but Belgium coach Marc Wilmots dismissed such labels.

"There is no such thing," said Wilmots. "It's a tough draw – nothing more. Our first match against Italy will be the toughest, but I don't think Italy will be happy to have drawn us either."

Group F will see Iceland, playing in their first major tournament finals, take on Cristiano Ronaldo's Portugal, Austria and Hungary. The Icelanders will not be fazed. As co-coach Heimir Hallgrímsson said: "We are probably most pleased with being one of the last teams to play. That gives us a chance to get into the spirit of the finals."

Not only has the number of teams (and groups) been expanded, the prize money on offer has also been raised. The total cash on offer is €301 million, an increase of more than 50 per cent from €196 million four years ago.

The winners can earn a maximum €27 million compared with €23.5 million in Poland and Ukraine. Each team will receive €8 million merely for turning up. After that come match bonuses in the group stage of €1 million for a win and €500,000 for a draw. Playing in the second round would earn a team €1.5 million with €2.5 million in the quarter-finals and €4 million in the semi-finals. The runners-up will earn a further €5 million with the winners taking away €8 million – and, of course, the glory.

Chapter 2
EURO 2016
Qualifiers

THE FINALIST NATIONS AT UEFA EURO 2016
EMERGED FROM A THRILLING QUALIFYING
COMPETITION INVOLVING 53 COUNTRIES
BATTLING TO JOIN HOSTS FRANCE.
THEIR ROUTE COMPRISED A TOTAL OF
268 MATCHES, IN WHICH 694 GOALS WERE
REGISTERED. ENGLAND WAS THE ONLY
NATION TO WIN ALL OF THEIR GROUP MATCHES,
WHILE THEY, ROMANIA, AUSTRIA AND ITALY
WERE ALL UNDEFEATED. POLAND'S ROBERT
LEWANDOWSKI WAS THE 13-GOAL TOP SCORER.

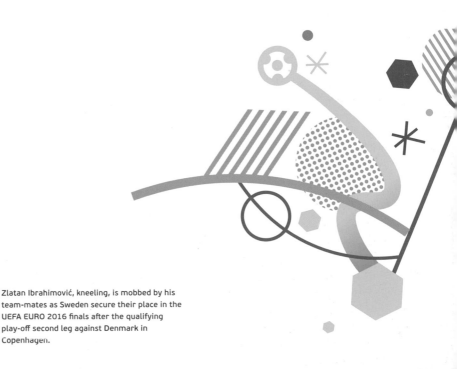

Zlatan Ibrahimović, kneeling, is mobbed by his
team-mates as Sweden secure their place in the
UEFA EURO 2016 finals after the qualifying
play-off second leg against Denmark in
Copenhagen.

GROUP A

The greatest surprise of the qualifying tournament was the Netherlands' failure to qualify. In 2014, the Dutchmen had finished third at the FIFA World Cup finals in Brazil. But a management handover from Louis Van Gaal to Guus Hiddink, coupled with a need to rebuild, proved a challenge too far.

The writing was on the wall for the Dutch from the first round, when they lost 2–1 away to the Czech Republic in Prague. They came within minutes of taking what would have been a creditable draw but a stoppage-time goal from Václav Pilař provided the Czechs with a victory that gave them not only the three points, but also a valuable injection of confidence.

The same day, almost unnoticed beyond the two nations involved, Iceland scored a decisive 3–0 win over Turkey, who then went on to lose 2–1 at home to the Czechs.

Meanwhile, Iceland went from strength to strength. Gylfi Sigurdsson struck the first of three goals away to Kazakhstan and then both goals in a 2–0 home win over the dispirited Netherlands.

The Icelanders then completed a surprising double over the Netherlands by winning 1–0 in Amsterdam. Sigurdsson converted the decisive penalty against a Dutch team who had just undergone a managerial change, with Danny Blind taking over the reins from Hiddink. The Czechs took happy advantage to push ahead at the top of the table with a 2–1 win over Kazakhstan and then a 2–1 win in Latvia.

Finally, Turkey sparked into life. Encouraged by a 1–1 draw in the Netherlands, they won 1–0 in Kazakhstan, drew 1–1 at home to

GROUP A	P	W	D	L	F	A	GD	Pts
Czech Republic	10	7	1	2	19	14	5	22
Iceland	10	6	2	2	17	6	11	20
Turkey	10	5	3	2	14	9	5	18
Netherlands	10	4	1	5	17	14	3	13
Kazakhstan	10	1	2	7	7	18	-11	5
Latvia	10	0	5	5	6	19	-13	5

Latvia and maintained their newfound momentum by defeating the Netherlands 3–0 in Konya.

The Turks' subsequent 2–0 win in the Czech Republic may not have toppled the Czechs from the top of the table but it did prove crucial to the outcome of the group. With Iceland heading for the runners-up spot, third place and entry to the play-offs rested on the outcome of the final round of matches.

The Netherlands needed to win at home to the already qualified Czechs and hope that the Turks lost to Iceland. Nothing went right for the Dutch. Turkey won 1–0 and the Dutch lost 3–2 with Robin van Persie's own goal providing what proved the Czechs' winner.

BELOW: Iceland's Gylfi Sigurdsson celebrates after scoring from the penalty spot for the crucial goal against the Netherlands in their Group A qualifying match in Amsterdam.

GROUP B

Belgium, profiting from the experience their outstanding young team had gained at the 2014 FIFA World Cup, were always clear favourites to lead the way into the UEFA EURO 2016 finals. Unpredictable, however, was the manner in which the race for the supporting slots was resolved, with Wales, Israel and Bosnia and Herzegovina all fighting for the final automatic qualifying berth.

Wales had been improving steadily over recent years under the managements of John Toshack, Gary Speed and then Chris Coleman, while the Bosnians had enjoyed a lively outing at the FIFA World Cup in Brazil. The Israelis could always be guaranteed to make life awkward for all their opponents.

Wales, in particular, had gained renewed respect, primarily because their attack now boasted the world's most expensive player in roaming forward Gareth Bale, who had cost Real Madrid €100 million when he moved from Tottenham in the summer of 2013.

Bale lived up to his billing by scoring both goals when the Welsh opened their campaign with a narrow 2–1 away win against Andorra. They were further encouraged, the same evening, to learn that the Bosnians had lost 2–1 at home to Cyprus.

Belgium marked their entry into the campaign with a 6–0 home win over Andorra, but then stumbled with two successive draws. First, it took a late goal from Radja Nainggolan to rescue a 1–1 draw against Bosnia and Herzegovina in Zenica and then they were held at home in a highly competitive goalless duel with Wales.

Coleman's men underlined their potential when they defeated

GROUP B								
	P	W	D	L	F	A	GD	Pts
Belgium	10	7	2	1	24	5	19	23
Wales	10	6	3	1	11	4	7	21
Bos./Herzegovina	10	5	2	3	17	12	5	17
Israel	10	4	1	5	16	14	2	13
Cyprus	10	4	0	6	16	17	−1	12
Andorra	10	0	0	10	4	36	−32	0

ABOVE: Gareth Bale leaps to head the only goal Wales required as they defeated Cyprus in Nicosia in their Group B qualifying match in September 2015.

Belgium in Cardiff. Inevitably, it was Bale who scored the decisive single goal midway through the first half.

Simultaneously, the Bosnians put their inconsistent campaign back on track with a 3–1 home win over Israel thanks to two goals from Edin Višća. However, they then lost 3–1 in Belgium. A 2–0 win over Wales came too late to dislodge the Red Dragons from runners-up spot and the Bosnians had to be satisfied "merely" with third place and entry into the play-offs.

GROUP C

The commanding manner in which Spain won Group C reassured coach Vicente del Bosque and the European champions' fans. La Roja had won the European title in 2008 and 2012, but the loss of their world crown in 2014 had prompted a rethink about personnel and style. Nine wins out of ten in the qualifying campaign suggested that answers both had been sought and had been found.

Slovakia and Ukraine eased in behind Spain, as runners-up and third-placed nations, with Belarus, Luxembourg and Macedonia trailing in the trio's wake.

Spain started in perfect form. They put their FIFA World Cup depression behind them with a 5–1 defeat of Macedonia in Valencia. Significantly, Paco Alcácer from Valencia CF, a leading member of a new breakthrough generation, struck the first goal.

The 22-year-old would end up as the group's five-goal joint leading scorer, filling a role that had troubled del Bosque ever since injuries had disrupted attacking predecessors such as Fernando Torres and 59-goal record marksman David Villa. Spain had taken refuge in the "false No.9" tactic, but needed something new – Alcácer had arrived at precisely the right moment.

The victory over Macedonia, almost on its own, left little doubt that the issue in Group C would be all about who would finish second in the table behind Spain to secure their place in the finals. Spain would go on to drop points only once, a 2–1 defeat away to Slovakia in Zilina in their second game. They scored 23 goals and conceded only three to finish five points clear of their nearest pursuers.

Slovakia had struck a decisive blow by winning their opening

GROUP C	P	W	D	L	F	A	GD	Pts
Spain	10	9	0	1	23	3	20	27
Slovakia	10	7	1	2	17	8	9	22
Ukraine	10	6	1	3	14	4	10	19
Belarus	10	3	2	5	8	14	−6	11
Luxembourg	10	1	1	8	6	27	−21	4
Macedonia	10	1	1	8	6	18	−12	4

ABOVE: Luxembourg are beaten 4–0 in Logrono as Spain's latest hero, centre-forward Paco Alcácer, scores one of his five Group C goals.

game away to dangerous Ukraine. In fact, the Slovaks continued their winning streak for a year, until they succumbed to a revenge victory for Spain in Oviedo.

The defeat to the Spanish snapped Slovak confidence. They were held at home by pursuing Ukraine and, surprisingly, lost at home to Belarus. However, they still qualified for the finals in France. Ukraine went on to finish third, regretting the high cost of that opening defeat at home to Slovakia.

GROUP D

Even when the draw was made, long before their triumph at the FIFA World Cup in Brazil in the summer of 2014, Germany were favourites to win qualifying Group D. But they did not have it all their own way before eventually scrambling to top spot ahead of Poland and the Republic of Ireland.

The particular novelty in this group was the presence of Gibraltar, the latest national association welcomed into membership of UEFA at the European federation's congress in London in the spring of 2013. Less welcoming was the outcome of their competitive debut, a 7–0 defeat at the hands of Poland and four-goal Robert Lewandowski.

Simultaneously, Germany opened their account with a hard-earned 2–1 home win over Scotland in Dortmund, with a brace from Lewandowski's FC Bayern Munich club-mate Thomas Müller.

A month later, Poland strode ahead of their neighbours at the top of the group when they defeated Joachim Löw's world champions 2–0

GROUP D	P	W	D	L	F	A	GD	Pts
Germany	10	7	1	2	24	9	15	22
Poland	10	6	3	1	33	10	23	21
Rep. Ireland	10	5	3	2	19	7	12	18
Scotland	10	4	3	3	22	12	10	15
Georgia	10	3	0	7	10	16	–6	9
Gibraltar	10	0	0	10	2	56	–54	0

in Warsaw. The heroes of the evening were Arek Milik and Sebastian Mila who struck the two second-half goals.

In their next match, the Germans managed only a 1–1 home draw against the visiting Republic of Ireland, who were thrilled to see a performance of outstanding commitment rewarded with an equaliser deep into stoppage time from John O'Shea.

Next it was Poland's turn to be surprised when they were held 2–2 at home by Scotland. Gordon Strachan's visitors even led 2–1 heading into the closing stages of the match. Milik came to the rescue for the Poles, who were then held 1–1 in Ireland. Like the Germans before them, Poland were denied victory by a stoppage-time Irish equaliser, this time from Shane Long.

That set the stage for the decisive closing rounds in which Germany, at last, regained much of their poise. One goal from Müller and two from Bayern team-mate Mario Götze earned a 3–1 win over Poland in Frankfurt. Muller struck twice more in victory over Scotland and the first goal – from the penalty spot – in the concluding 2–1 win over Georgia that saw Germany finish the campaign a solitary point ahead of the Poles.

Polish consolation, apart from automatic qualification, was seeing Lewandowski hailed as the top qualifying marksman with 13 goals, equalling David Healy's record for Northern Ireland in 2008.

BELOW: Forward Thomas Müller (No. 13) holds off a challenge from Poland's Kamil Glik during Germany's 3–1 victory in Frankfurt.

GROUP E

England, unlike many other qualifying hopefuls, led from start to finish to become only the fifth national side to qualify for a modern UEFA European Football Championship with a 100 per cent record. They won every one of their ten matches with captain Wayne Rooney setting a national team scoring record along the way.

The pattern was set from the outset and England's visit to Basel, a challenging opening for manager Roy Hodgson. In 1994, he had led the Swiss to the FIFA World Cup finals for the first time in 28 years. But the latest FIFA World Cup in Brazil had been a difficult experience for Hodgson and England. They had been eliminated after two games and within little more than a week, while the Swiss had reached the second round.

In the St Jakob-Park, however, England were more sure-footed in defence and more decisive in attack. Danny Welbeck scored twice to provide Hodgson with a secure

GROUP E	P	W	D	L	F	A	GD	Pts
England	10	10	0	0	31	3	28	30
Switzerland	10	7	0	3	24	8	16	21
Slovenia	10	5	1	4	18	11	7	16
Estonia	10	3	1	6	4	9	-5	10
Lithuania	10	3	1	6	7	18	-11	10
San Marino	10	0	1	9	1	36	-35	1

foundation for his team evolution.

The return against Switzerland, the following September, was a party day at Wembley. The previous Saturday, Rooney, during a 6–0 win in San Marino, had opened the scoring with a penalty – his 49th England goal, equalling the record set by

Sir Bobby Charlton between 1958 and 1970. England defeated the Swiss (who would go on to claim the runners-up spot in the group) 2–0 to become the first team to qualify for the finals, with Rooney becoming the country's record marksman following an 84th-minute penalty. Hodgson's men thus reached France with three matches to spare, having gone 12 matches unbeaten for the first time since 1996.

Hodgson hailed Rooney's exploits as an "amazing achievement", but offered cautionary words too, saying: "Now the most important thing we have to do is make sure we keep improving our performances because we didn't play as well as we could have done."

Elsewhere in the group, Slovenia maintained their progress by finishing in third place by edging fourth-placed Estonia 1–0. San Marino finished sixth although, along the way, Matteo Vitaioli ended their run of 34 away games without a goal in a 2–1 defeat by Lithuania.

BELOW: Danny Welbeck (9) and Wayne Rooney outpace Switzerland's Johan Djourou as England open their Group E qualifying campaign with a 2–0 victory at the St Jakob-Park in Basel.

GROUP F

Northern Ireland qualified for the UEFA European Football Championship finals for the first time in their history and for the climactic stage of a major tournament for the first time since their appearance at the 1986 FIFA World Cup in Mexico. Romania followed them to France, with a revived Hungary clinching the play-off spot.

The group was one of the most unpredictable, though Greece were expected to play a decisive role. They had proved their pedigree not only a decade earlier by winning UEFA EURO 2004 but also by coming within a penalty shootout of a place in the quarter-finals at the FIFA World Cup in Brazil.

Greece entered the UEFA EURO 2016 qualifiers under new management. Fernando Santos had left after the FIFA World Cup and was succeeded by the veteran Italian Claudio Ranieri.

All his early positivity soon faded, however. Greece lost their opening qualifier 1–0 at home to Romania, rescued a 1–1 draw in Finland, but then lost at home again, this time by 2–0 to Northern Ireland. A further home defeat, 1–0 against the Faroe Islands, was followed within hours by Ranieri's departure. It was only the Faroe Islands' 20th victory since entering the international arena in 1988.

At the top of the table, by this time, were Romania. They had won three of their four initial games including, importantly, a 2–0 victory over the Irish who had been early leaders. Paul Papp scored both goals in the National Arena in Bucharest. Hungary, after a slow start, had also started to put wins together.

Heading into the home stretch, in September 2015, Romania held the advantage after forcing a goalless draw in Belfast. But then they were held to three successive draws by Hungary, Greece and Finland. The Irish took advantage to regain top spot, which they maintained, despite being held 1–1 in their concluding visit to Finland. Kyle Lafferty finished as the group's seven-goal top scorer.

Romania regained winning form with a 3–0 win in the Faroe Islands, but victory was too late to lift them top of the table. At least, however, it provided the insurance they needed to attain second place.

GROUP F								
	P	W	D	L	F	A	GD	Pts
N Ireland	10	6	3	1	16	8	8	21
Romania	10	5	5	0	11	2	9	20
Hungary	10	4	4	2	11	9	2	16
Finland	10	3	3	4	9	10	-1	12
Faroe Islands	10	2	0	8	6	17	-11	6
Greece	10	1	3	6	7	14	-7	6

BELOW: Kyle Lafferty (right) battles for possession with Greek defender Kostas Stafylidis during Northern Ireland's 2-0 Group F victory in Piraeus.

Wayne Rooney (10) celebrates with Harry Kane after scoring for England with a penalty against Switzerland in a Group E qualifying match at Wembley in September 2015. It was his 50th goal for his country and he passed Sir Bobby's Charlton's old record.

GROUP G

Austria and Russia forged their paths to France with Sweden pushed back to third place, despite the inspirational star status of Zlatan Ibrahimović. The Paris Saint-Germain striker finished up as the group's eight-goal joint top scorer along with the impressive young Artem Dzyuba from Russia's FC Zenit.

Dzyuba struck his first goal in the 4–0 victory over Liechtenstein with which Russia launched their qualifying campaign. They followed up with a satisfying 1–1 draw away to Sweden. The positive start was important for Russian confidence after their early exit from the FIFA World Cup in Brazil and the awareness that their status as 2018 hosts brought international attention with every outing.

Montenegro and Moldova were expected to play dangerous roles with their potential for an upset, but the greatest surprise was the re-emergence of Austria, one of the greatest of European football nations in the first half of the 20th century.

After being held 1–1 at home in Vienna in their opening game, Marcel Koller's team won all their succeeding nine games to become one of the first nations to book their ticket to France. They were top scorers in the group with 22 goals, conceding only five. Widely travelled Marc Janko was their seven-goal leading marksman, aided by significant contributions from David Alaba (four) plus Marko Arnautovic and Martin Harnik (with three apiece).

Heading into the closing stages of the qualifying campaign, Sweden held all the cards to follow the Austrians directly to France. They had 12 points, four more than a Russia team now under new management after CSKA's Leonid Slutsky had been

GROUP G	P	W	D	L	F	A	GD	Pts
Austria	10	9	1	0	22	5	17	28
Russia	10	6	2	2	21	5	16	20
Sweden	10	5	3	2	15	9	6	18
Montenegro**	10	3	2	5	10	13	–3	11
Liechtenstein	10	1	2	7	2	26	–24	5
Moldova	10	0	2	8	4	16	–12	2

**Montenegro's home match against Russia awarded 3–0 to Russia after match was abandoned after 67 minutes

appointed, on a part-time basis, to succeed Fabio Capello.

Crucially, the opening autumn match brought Sweden to Moscow, where Dzyuba struck the only, winning goal. Three days later, while Russia were running up seven goals in Liechtenstein, Sweden were succumbing 4–1 at home to Austria

– their only goal, from Ibrahimović, arriving only in stoppage time.

It left Russia in pole position to secure the runners-up spot and they made no mistake with wins away to Moldova and at home to Montenegro. Even though Sweden won their own last two games, they had to be content with a place in the play-offs

BELOW: Russia's new star, Artem Dzyuba struggles to find a way between Montenegro's Mladen Kašćelan (16) and Esteban Saveljich, but the Russians still went on to win 2–0 in Moscow.

GROUP H

Italy and Croatia qualified for the finals in France even though the competition went right to the closing round of matches when Norway, who ultimately finished third, entered with the possible prospect of finishing in top spot. In the event results went against them but it was desperately close.

Italy, under new manager Antonio Conte who had succeeded Cesare Prandelli following the 2014 FIFA World Cup, got off to a winning start in Norway. Goals from Simone Zaza and Leonardo Bonucci would ultimately prove even more important than they appeared at the time.

Italy and Croatia were opening pacesetters in the group with three successive victories each and they duly then ended up all-square at 1–1 in Milan the first time they met. Croatia then seized the group leadership by defeating Norway 5–1 while the Italians were struggling to rescue a 2–2 draw in Bulgaria.

The Poljud stadium in Split then saw Croatia and Italy draw their return match, following another 1–1 draw, but the hosts would ultimately forfeit the point gained after being sanctioned by UEFA for racist behaviour by their fans. They were also ordered to play their next two competitive home matches behind closed doors.

It proved a turning point in the outcome of the group. Croatia drew in Azerbaijan and lost in Norway, while Italy were snatching narrow 1–0 wins over Malta and Bulgaria. Graziano Pellè and Daniele De Rossi scored the respective winning goals that secured Italy's qualification with one round to spare.

The Azzurri were still under

GROUP H	P	W	D	L	F	A	GD	Pts
Italy	10	7	3	0	16	7	9	24
Croatia**	10	6	3	1	20	5	15	20
Norway	10	6	1	3	13	10	3	19
Bulgaria	10	3	2	5	9	12	-3	11
Azerbaijan	10	1	3	6	7	18	-11	6
Malta	10	0	2	8	3	16	-13	2

**Croatia deducted one point after charges for racist behaviour in the match against Italy

ABOVE: Match-winner Graziano Pellè led Italy to a 2–1 victory over Norway in the concluding match of Group H in Rome, his 82nd-minute goal settling the match.

pressure in their final game, however. Norway came to Rome knowing that if they won and Croatia lost in Malta then they would go through to the finals as runners-up. Croatia took the lead in Malta but could not extend it, and when Alexander Tettey put

Norway ahead in Rome the visitors' dream remained alive.

Only until the closing quarter of an hour. Alessandro Florenzi and Pellè struck twice in nine minutes for Italy, and a relieved Croatia were able to celebrate, after all, in Ta'Qali.

GROUP I

Cristiano Ronaldo, commander of a multiplicity of awards at national and international level, duly led Portugal back to the finals. He was five-goal top scorer in a group the Portuguese won with a decisive seven-point advantage over Albania, who wrote their own chapter of football history by reaching the finals of a major tournament for the first time.

The unusual factor about Group I was that it contained five nations, one fewer than the other eight groups. The draw had been designed so that France could be included in the fixture schedule and thus be guaranteed European opposition in the friendly matches that would comprise their preparations to play host in June 2016.

Once they had overcome the shock of losing their opening match 1–0 at home to Albania, Portugal's progress was never in doubt. Bekim Balaj volleyed the second-half winning goal, his first for his country. The Portuguese federation reacted by replacing Paulo Bento as national

GROUP I	P	W	D	L	F	A	GD	Pts
Portugal	8	7	0	1	11	5	6	21
Albania	8	4	2	2	10	5	5	14
Denmark	8	3	3	2	8	5	3	12
Serbia	8	2	1	5	8	13	−5	4
Armenia	8	0	2	6	5	14	−9	2

coach with Fernando Santos and, under him, Portugal won every one of their remaining seven games, albeit scoring a comparatively meagre 11 goals.

The central duel for the ultimate outcome of the other places rested between Albania and former European champions Denmark.

This pair reached end of the 2014–15 season level on ten points, but Albania held a narrow advantage by dint of having played only four games. Albania then benefited during the summer from a ruling at the Court of Arbitration for Sport. The CAS awarded them a 3–0 victory from a tie against Serbia in Belgrade the previous October that was abandoned because of violence.

Denmark had the opportunity to regain lost ground when Albania came to Copenhagen in September. Instead, Albania held out for a goalless draw. When Denmark lost 1–0 in Portugal in their last group game, they remained in second place but knew they were vulnerable.

Albania had still to play their own last game away to an Armenia, who were without a win in the entire campaign. A 3–0 victory for the visitors lifted them into second place, two points above Morten Olsen's Danes who were thus pushed down into the play-offs.

BELOW: Skipper Cristiano Ronaldo shoots for goal in Group I table-topping Portugal's 1–0 win against Albania in Elbasan in September 2015.

THE PLAY-OFFS

The play-off system was more significant than ever for UEFA EURO 2016. The expansion of the finals from 16 to 24 teams had opened the scope for more teams to reach France, but it also increased the need to ensure a competitive edge throughout the qualifying tournament.

Eight of the nine groups provided a third-placed team for the play-offs. The one exception was Group A, from which Turkey proved the highest-ranked of the third-placed teams and thus were granted automatic qualification. This was computed from a mini league of the results of all nine teams, but excluding those against any sixth-placed country.

The eight remaining third-placed teams were then seeded into two pots according to their UEFA national team coefficient rankings and were drawn to play each other over two legs over one match-week: 12–14 and 15–17 November. In the event Bosnia and Herzegovina were the only "top pot" team not to reach the finals.

Hungary's success in regaining a place on the international stage after 30 years was widely welcomed ... apart from play-off rivals Norway. The Hungarians edged the first leg away in Oslo with a debut goal from László Kleinheisler, though they were fortunate when Norway's André Helland headed against the bar from close range in the closing stages. Hungary clinched their place in the finals when they won 2–1 at home in a game that saw Norwegian midfielder Markus Henriksen score at both ends.

Bosnia and Herzegovina dominated their home first leg against the Republic of Ireland, but lost their attacking way in the fog in Zenica.

PLAY-OFF RESULTS			
Ukraine v Slovenia	2–0,	1–1	(3–1 on agg)
Sweden v Denmark	2–1,	2–2	(4–3 on agg)
Bosnia-Herzegovina v **Rep. Ireland**	1–1,	0–2	(1–3 on agg)
Norway v **Hungary**	0–1,	1–2	(1–3 on agg)

ABOVE: Jon Walters shoots the Republic of Ireland ahead with a penalty in the second leg of the play-off against Bosnia-Herzegovina in Dublin. Ireland won 2–0 on the night and 3–1 on aggregate.

Only after midfielder Robbie Brady shot the Irish into an unlikely 82nd-minute lead did Edin Džeko find his way through for an equaliser.

Brady had an outstanding match in the second leg too. Jon Walters, back after suspension, shot Ireland ahead from a first-half penalty awarded for handball. Bosnia battled back and appeared the more threatening before Walters struck again, conclusively.

Having played co-hosts in 2012, Ukraine returned to the finals with a 3–1 aggregate victory over Slovenia, which was not as clear as the scoreline appeared. Andriy Yarmolenko and Yevhen Seleznyov struck in each half in Lviv, but Slovenia led for almost all of the return leg in Maribor through captain Bostjan Cesar. The hosts threw caution to the wind in the closing minutes only to be caught, fatally, on the break by Yarmolenko.

Sweden had Zlatan Ibrahimović to thank for driving them through against Nordic neighbours Denmark. He struck their second goal in a 2–1 home win in Stockholm and then twice more to put Sweden 2–0 ahead in Copenhagen. Denmark hit back for a 2–2 draw, but it proved too little too late.

GROUP C

- GERMANY
- UKRAINE
- POLAND
- NORTHERN IRELAND

P D

PAIN
ZECH REPUBLIC
URKEY
ROATIA

UEFA
EURO2016
FRANCE

GROUP E

- BELGIUM
- ITALY
- REPUBLIC OF IRELAND
- SWEDEN

Chapter 3
Meet the Teams

OUTSTANDING TEAMS AND OUTSTANDING PLAYERS WILL SEIZE THE ATTENTION ONCE UEFA EURO 2016 KICKS OFF ON 10 JUNE. ALL LAST TIME'S SEMI-FINALISTS ARE BACK WITH TITLE-WINNING AMBITIONS FROM CHAMPIONS SPAIN, TO ITALY, GERMANY AND PORTUGAL. THIS PROMISES QUALITY IN FRANCE AS A PRODUCT OF BOTH CONSISTENCY AND EXPERIENCE FROM THE LIKES OF ANDRES INIESTA, GIGI BUFFON, THOMAS MÜLLER AND CRISTIANO RONALDO – PLUS THE NEW STARS CERTAIN TO SHINE ON EUROPE'S BIGGEST STAGE.

The draw for any major tournament finals is a giant step towards the start. Every country knows who, where and when they will be playing in the first round group stage and can start the serious preparations for each opponent, to say nothing of confirming travel, training and accommodation plans away from their training bases. All that is now left is for the captain to lift the Henri Delaunay Trophy on 10 July 2016.

GROUP A
FRANCE

France, hosting the climax of the UEFA European Football Championship for the third time, will carry the hopes of the nation as they seek to match their triumph of 1984, the last time they staged the finals. Coach Didier Deschamps and his squad will inevitably be among the favourites to lift the Henri Delaunay Trophy in the Stade de France on 10 July.

COACH
DIDIER DESCHAMPS

Didier Deschamps has been working hard, since his appointment in succession to Laurent Blanc after UEFA EURO 2012, to convert his success as a player, captain and leader into similar achievements as national coach. Deschamps was a feisty, hard-working midfielder who wore the armband with pride when he led France to glory at both the 1998 FIFA World Cup and the 2000 UEFA European Championship. He scored four goals in 103 internationals between 1989 and 2000 while winning club titles at home and abroad with Nantes, Marseille, Bordeaux, Juventus, Chelsea and Valencia. After retiring as a player, Deschamps coached Monaco, Juventus and Marseille.

France have a proud football history both on and off the pitch. Frenchmen such as Robert Guerin, Jules Rimet, Henri Delaunay and Gabriel Hanot all played crucial roles, respectively, in the creation of the game's world federation FIFA, the FIFA World Cup, UEFA and its European Championship, as well as what is now known as the UEFA Champions League.

On the pitch, it was Frenchman Lucien Laurent who scored the first goal at the inaugural FIFA World Cup finals in 1930 and France who hosted the first European Football

Championship – then known as the Nations Cup – in 1960.

Les Bleus finished fourth on that occasion, but the next time they hosted the finals, in 1984, they won the European crown. France were hosts of the 1998 FIFA World Cup and followed up another victory on home soil with a second UEFA EURO triumph in neighbouring Belgium and the Netherlands two years later.

Since then, France's best achievement is runners-up, on penalties, to Italy at the 2006 FIFA World Cup. Didier Deschamps, who

BELOW: When France hosted UEFA EURO 1984, and FIFA World Cup 1998, *Les Bleus* won the tournaments. Will goalkeeper and captain Hugo Lloris lift the trophy at the end of UEFA EURO 2016?

STAR PLAYER
PAUL POGBA

POSITION: **Midfielder** · CLUB: **Juventus (Italy)** · AGE: **23**
BORN: **15 March 1993, Lagny-sur-Marne, France**
INTERNATIONAL DEBUT: **22 March 2013 v Georgia**
CAPS: **25** · GOALS: **5**

Paul Pogba is one of the brightest prospects in European football, who possesses remarkable power and poise for a player still with a decade's achievement ahead of him. Pogba was signed as a 16-year-old by Manchester United but, for all his prowess with the French youth teams, it was not until he moved on to Juventus in 2012 that he made an impact on European football. Nicknamed "The Octopus" for his long-striding style, Pogba anchored three successive Serie A triumphs and starred in Juve's run to the 2015 UEFA Champions League final. On the national team stage, he was a FIFA World Under-20 champion in 2013 and was voted best young player at the 2014 FIFA World Cup in Brazil.

captained *Les Bleus* to glory in 1998 and 2000, now coaches the national team and wants to use home advantage to win another major title.

Two years ago, France reached the quarter-finals of the FIFA World Cup in Brazil before losing 1–0 to eventual champions Germany. Since then, Deschamps has maintained the core of the team that, with two years' more experience, should be capable of going deep into the tournament.

France have prepared for "their" finals without playing any competitive matches since 2014 (the hosts qualify automatically for the finals), but Deschamps has left no doubt in his players' minds that they have been competing, in every game, for their place in the squad in June.

For the most part he has used a 4-3-3 system, but has experimented with shapes and substitutions in a series of quality friendly matches against the likes of Spain, Belgium, Portugal, Brazil and England.

Hugo Lloris has been one of the best and most reliable goalkeepers in Europe for a decade. A three-times Goalkeeper of the Year in France, while playing for Nice and Lyon, he then moved to England's Premier League with Tottenham in 2012.

In front of him, Lens product Raphael Varane, now at Real Madrid, is considered to be one of the classiest central defenders in the European game. Ahead of them is a solid midfield anchored by Paul Pogba from Juventus.

Pogba failed to achieve an early career breakthrough at Manchester United, but capitalised on a move to Italy with Juventus in style. He was official man of the match when France defeated Nigeria 2–0 in the second round of the FIFA World Cup in 2014 and was outstanding in Juventus' run to the final of the UEFA Champions League in 2015.

Deschamps no longer has the attacking danger of Franck Ribéry at his service, but the likes of Antoine Griezmann, Olivier Giroud and Anthony Martial will provide him with plenty of firepower.

Griezmann is one of Europe's most highly-rated wingers. Yet he never played senior club football in France, joining Spain's Real Sociedad after impressing in a youth tournament in 2005 when still only 14. He moved to Atlético de Madrid in 2014 for a fee of €24 million and was immediately a Spanish Supercup winner.

Centre-forward Giroud has gained plenty of experience with Arsenal, while Manchester United's Anthony Martial, who became world football's most expensive teenager when he left Monaco for Old Trafford last summer, has shown plenty of promise.

With such talent running through the team, France are one of the prime favourites to light up the tournament.

FRANCE AT THE UEFA EURO FINALS

1960	Fourth place
1964	Did not qualify
1968	Did not qualify
1972	Did not qualify
1976	Did not qualify
1980	Did not qualify
1984	WINNERS
1988	Did not qualify
1992	Group stage
1996	Semi-finals
2000	WINNERS
2004	Quarter-final
2008	Group stage
2012	Quarter-final

ROMANIA

Romania have won only once in their four previous appearances at the UEFA EURO finals (when they reached the 2000 quarter-finals), but the robust security of a defence that conceded only two goals in their qualifying campaign indicates that this is a team which will be hard to beat in France – and one that will be determined to prove that they have match-winning ambitions of their own.

COACH

ANGHEL IORDANESCU

Anghel Iordănescu's remarkable career has seen him win top honours both as a player and manager as well as become a member of Romania's National Senate. Born in Bucharest on 4 May 1950, he spent most of his senior playing career with Steaua, and was part of the team that became Romania's only UEFA European Champions Cup winners in 1986. Later, at the 1994 FIFA World Cup during the first of his three stints as national coach, he led Romania to a best-ever quarter-finals place. In 2008, Iordanescu announced his retirement from football to concentrate on a political career, but he was persuaded to return to national team duty in the autumn of 2014 to succeed Victor Pițurcă.

Romania have appeared at three of the last five UEFA EURO finals (missing out in 2004 and 2012), and their regular appearances on European football's biggest stage is a testament to both their consistency and talent.

Veteran coach Anghel Iordănescu, who knows all about tournament pressures from his own playing days, brings his players to France having finished as runners-up behind Northern Ireland in Group F of the qualifying competition.

On one hand, Romania made harder work of qualifying than they might have expected. On the other hand, however, Iordănescu was forced to construct a squad almost from scratch after the disappointments of failing to qualify for both UEFA EURO 2012 and the 2014 FIFA World Cup finals.

They began their campaign soundly, with victories away to Greece and Finland either side of a 1–1 home draw with Hungary. Further successes at home to Northern Ireland and then the Faroe Islands established Romania as halfway favourites to win the group, possibly with a match or two to spare.

However, as Romania's problems in attack grew – they drew their next three games, against Hungary, Greece

BELOW: Romania's squad wants to make the country's sixth appearance at the UEFA European Football Championships finals better than others as they have yet to enjoy a knock-out round victory.

STAR PLAYER
RĂZVAN RAŢ

POSITION: **Defender** • CLUB: **Rayo Vallecano de Madrid (Spain)**
AGE: **34** • BORN: **26 May 1981, Piatra-Olt, Romania**
INTERNATIONAL DEBUT: **8 February 2002, v France**
CAPS: **107** • GOALS: **2**

Răzvan Raţ will be one of the most experienced defenders appearing in the UEFA EURO 2016 finals. He made his debut for Romania in 2002, against France and was appointed national team captain. Leading by robust example, Raţ led his team at the UEFA EURO 2008 finals. He is one of only five Romanians to have reached a century of international appearances, winning his 100th cap against Finland in October 2014. Raţ's club career successes have included eight league titles (two with Rapid Bucharest in Romania and six with Shakhtar Donetsk in Ukraine), national cups in Romania and Ukraine as well as the UEFA Cup with Shakhtar when they defeated Germany's Werder Bremen in 2009.

and Finland – the Irish took advantage and overtook them to snatch top spot in the group. In the end, Romania had to win their last match, away to the Faroe Islands, to ensure qualification. Two goals from Constantin Budescu and another from Alexandru Maxim gave them a 3–0 victory to book their ticket to France. It was a vital win for a country which had embraced football long before most of its Balkan neighbours.

King Carol I was a football fanatic and he prompted the formation of Romania's football federation in 1908. The enthusiasm of another king, Carol II, also ensured Romania were one of four European nations to enter the inaugural FIFA World Cup in 1930.

Early round exits were all they had to show from the inaugural World Cups in 1930, 1934 and 1938, but it was not until 1970 that Romania returned to the world stage. The domestic game was now dominated by the Bucharest rivals, Steaua and Dinamo, and they provided the nucleus of the national team that reached the UEFA EURO finals for the first time in 1984.

Romania then reached three consecutive FIFA World Cup finals from 1990 to 1998 and the UEFA EURO finals in both 1996 and 2000.

This team boasted the inspiration of their greatest player in schemer Gheorghe Hagi, but lacked luck. They were eliminated on penalties at both the 1990 and 1994 FIFA World Cups. At UEFA EURO 2000, they finally won a match (3–2 against England), but then lost to Italy in the quarter-finals after Hagi had been shown a red card.

In UEFA EURO 2008, Romania were eliminated in the first round and the bleak statistic of one win in 13 games at the finals is a record they intend to improve in France.

Defence holds the key. Romania conceded a competition-best two goals in their ten qualifiers, with Fiorentina's Ciprian Tătărusanu a secure goalkeeper behind a solid back line featuring captain Răzvan Raţ, Napoli's Vlad Chicheş, Steaua's Paul Papp and Toulouse's Dragoş Grigore.

Gabriel Torje has provided versatility on the flanks, bringing into play all the guile he has learned from club football not only in Romania but also in Italy, Spain and Turkey. Maxim, who now plays his football in Germany with VfB Stuttgart, has proved himself a midfielder who is adept at both creating and scoring goals.

Bogdan Stancu, from Turkey's Gençlerbirliği, is the leading marksman among Romania's current clutch of attackers. His two goals in the vital 2–0 away victory over Finland in the qualifying campaign provided the springboard from which his country hope to go on to even greater things at the finals.

ROMANIA AT THE UEFA EURO FINALS

1960	Did not qualify
1964	Did not qualify
1968	Did not qualify
1972	Did not qualify
1976	Did not qualify
1980	Did not qualify
1984	Group stage
1988	Did not qualify
1992	Did not qualify
1996	Group stage
2000	Quarter-final
2004	Did not qualify
2008	Group stage
2012	Did not qualify

ALBANIA

Albania have never appeared in the finals of one of international football's major tournaments. Their presence at UEFA EURO 2016 illustrates perfectly the pace of sporting progress in what was once one of Europe's most reclusive nations. Now their great step into the football unknown is being led by an Italian coach and players from clubs all over Europe.

COACH
GIANNI DE BIASI

Italian Gianni De Biasi has made history by leading Albania to a major finals for the first time. De Biasi, born on 16 June 1956, in Treviso, began with Internazionale but did not play in a Serie A match for them. He moved on to Reggiana, Pescara, Brescia, Palermo and Vicenza before winding down his career in the lower divisions and turning to coaching. His first success came when he brought Torino back up into Serie A. De Biasi's first spell abroad was with Spain's Levante, before he was appointed by Albania in succession to Josip Kuže in December 2011. Taking Albania to France earned De Biasi and his players Albania's highest civilian award from President Bujar Nishani.

Albania are relative newcomers to international football. In the early days of the UEFA European Football Championship, the country's political isolation meant they did not always enter the tournament. Between 1954 and 1963 they played only one international friendly match, against the former German Democratic Republic (East Germany). They had effectively lost more than half a century of sporting potential because football was first organised in Albania in the early 1900s.

Foreign residents brought the game to the country, with the first formal club, Independencia, being launched in Shkoder. The first league championship, however – organised exclusively among foreigners – collapsed in chaos following the outbreak of the First World War.

It took the influence of various occupying forces in the 1920s to reintroduce the game, and this time the locals were encouraged to join in. In 1928, King Zog came to the throne and sports activities were, for the first time, recognised as a legitimate area of governmental concern. In 1930, a Sports Ministry was set up; two years later, a football federation was formed.

BELOW: Having qualified as Group I runners-up, Albania will step into the unknown as they make their UEFA EURO finals debut with a 11 June match against Switzerland in Lens.

STAR PLAYER
LORIK CANA

POSITION: **Defender** • CLUB: **Nantes (France)** • AGE: **32**
BORN: **27 July 1983, Pristina, Kosovo**
INTERNATIONAL DEBUT: **11 June 2003, v Switzerland**
CAPS: **88** • GOALS: **1**

Lorik Cana finally chose to play for Albania in 2003, having also been qualified for Switzerland and France. A conversation with the then-national coach Hans-Peter Briegel proved persuasive, and he made his debut as a substitute in a UEFA EURO 2004 qualifier. Though born in Kosovo, Cana was brought up in Switzerland before turning professional with Paris Saint-Germain FC. Initially a defensive midfielder, he gained huge experience of European football styles not only in France (where he has also played for Olympique de Marseille and FC Nantes), but also in England (Sunderland), Turkey (Galatasatray AŞ) and Italy (SS Lazio).

Sadly, political unrest in the Balkans meant the national team did not play their first international match, against neighbouring Yugoslavia, until 1946.

Several outstanding players from Albania, such as Riza Lushta, Loro Boriçi and Naim Kryeziu, played in Italy in the early 1940s. Then came Panajot Pano, a star of the 1950s and early 1960s whose son, Ledio, also became an international. After that came Sulejman Demollari, who, while at Dinamo Bucarest, was voted the best foreign player to play in Romania.

As the 1960s progressed, Albania became regular entrants in the qualifying rounds of the UEFA European Football Championship and also the FIFA World Cup. But the national team and clubs suffered from a vicious circle: a lack of international contact meant early elimination, which meant the game in the country failed to progress.

Finally, though, with UEFA EURO 2016 on the horizon, everything came together. Albania made the perfect start to their qualifying campaign, winning 1–0 away to Portugal, the greatest victory in their history. Striker Bekim Balaj, then playing in the Czech Republic with Slavia Prague, scored the historic goal.

A 1–1 draw with Denmark was followed by a 3–0 victory over Serbia in Belgrade, an away victory over Armenia and another draw with the Danes. Successive home defeats by Portugal and Serbia threatened to wreck Albania's breakthrough dream, but Denmark's subsequent defeat in Portugal offered them hope. Albania, needing to win in Armenia to seize their ticket to France, won 3–0 in Yerevan to clinch the runners-up spot in Group I behind Portugal.

Oddly, over the course of the eight qualifying games not one Albanian player scored more than a single goal. Six players scored once each and were aided by an own goal from Armenia's Kamo Hovhannisyan in that decisive last round of matches.

Manager Gianni De Biasi has had more restricted selection options than many other managers in the European finals, but the advantage of such limitations has been an enforced need to field a settled team, from regular goalkeeper Etrit Berisha to striker Sokol Çikalleshi.

Lorik Cana, Ansi Agolli and Andi Lila have been holding firm in defence for most of the last decade with Ervin Bulku – now playing his club football

back home with KF Tirana – in charge of midfield. Finding goals is the main challenge, however. Hamdi Salihi from KF Skënderbeu Korçë is their leading international marksman, with a dozen goals for his country.

He and his attacking colleagues will need to be at their sharpest if Albania are to score the goals they will need to spring another surprise in France.

ALBANIA AT THE UEFA EURO FINALS

1960	Did not enter
1964	Did not qualify
1968	Did not qualify
1972	Did not qualify
1976	Did not enter
1980	Did not enter
1984	Did not qualify
1988	Did not qualify
1992	Did not qualify
1996	Did not qualify
2000	Did not qualify
2004	Did not qualify
2008	Did not qualify
2012	Did not qualify

GROUP A
SWITZERLAND

Switzerland will have one of the most experienced of squads at UEFA EURO 2016, with many players who played in the second round of the 2014 FIFA World Cup. Coach Vladimir Petković has benefited from the foundation work laid by his predecessor, the now-retired Ottmar Hitzfeld. He hopes to be the first manager to take Switzerland to the knockout stages of the European Football Championship.

COACH
VLADIMIR PETKOVIĆ

Vladimir Petković had a tough act to follow when he took over from Ottmar Hitzfeld after the "Nati" had reached the second round of the 2014 FIFA World Cup before losing to Argentina. Hitzfeld had set a high standard, but Petković's initial task was accomplished decisively when a 7–0 win over San Marino secured a slot at UEFA EURO 2016. Petković, born in Sarajevo on 15 August 1963, played and coached more than a dozen clubs in the former Yugoslavia and Switzerland. He honed his coaching talents in Turkey and Italy, latterly with Lazio of Rome, before being asked to carry on where Hitzfeld had left off in Brazil.

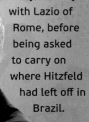

Although Switzerland has yet to win a trophy in an international competition, the country has always been at the forefront of world football. That is because both UEFA and the game's world governing body, FIFA, have their headquarters in the country.

A historic British influence is evident in the names of clubs such as Grasshopper Club (Zurich) and BSC Young Boys (Bern), but no Swiss club side has ever reached the final of a European competition.

The national side has fared slightly better, though, particularly in the 1920s and 1930s, when they finished as runners-up in the 1924 Olympic Games in Paris and reached the quarter-finals at both the 1934 and 1938 FIFA World Cups.

The most famous names of this era were the Abegglen brothers, Max and André, who scored more than 60 goals between them. The man responsible for this success was Karl Rappan, the "father" of Swiss football. He guided Switzerland to

BELOW: Switzerland's squad will want to end the country's long wait for a knock-out match in the UEFA European Championship after group stages exits in 1996, 2004 and 2008.

STAR PLAYER
XHERDAN SHAQIRI

POSITION: **Winger** • CLUB: **Stoke City (England)** • AGE: **24**
BORN: **10 October 1991, Gjilan, Kosovo**
INTERNATIONAL DEBUT: **3 March 2010, v Uruguay**
CAPS: **49** • GOALS: **17**

Xherdan Shaqiri is one of a number of players of Kosovar-Albanian background who have revived the national team – his family moved to Switzerland when he was one. Shaqiri came through FC Basel's youth teams, and he went on to win the league and cup double with them before leaving for German giants Bayern Munich in 2012 and then to England's Stoke City, via Internazionale in Italy. On the international stage, his speed and eye for goal caught "Nati" coach Ottmar Hitzfeld's attention, and he took him to both the 2010 and 2014 FIFA World Cups. In Brazil, Shaqiri's hat-trick against Honduras put Switzerland into the second round, in which they lost to eventual runners-up Argentina.

the finals of four of the first five FIFA World Cups played after the Second World War. Their best performance came in 1954 when, as hosts, they reached the quarter-finals.

After the 1966 FIFA World Cup, at which they did not win a game, the national side suffered a reversal of fortunes, and failed to qualify for the finals of a major tournament until the 1994 FIFA World Cup. They went on to make their UEFA EURO debut two years later. Switzerland have only missed one major tournament since 2004 – the UEFA EURO 2012 finals.

Under veteran coach Ottmar Hitzfeld, they reached the second round of the 2014 FIFA World Cup where they lost in extra-time to eventual runners-up Argentina. The nucleus of Hitzfeld's team has provided a solid foundation on which successor Vladimir Petković could build.

Not that they started well. Switzerland lost their opening two qualifying matches, to England and Slovenia, before putting together a run of four successive wins to secure qualifying momentum. In total, Switzerland won seven of their ten games, losing the other three, and ultimately finished as group runners-

up behind England, five points clear of third-placed Slovenia.

As at the FIFA World Cup in Brazil, the attacking onus fell on the shoulders of Xherdan Shaqiri. The 24-year-old was their leading marksman during qualification with four goals, one more than strikers Josip Drmic and Haris Seferovic.

Solid experience in defence was provided by Juventus' Stephan Lichtsteiner and Hamburg's Johan Djourou – with more than 140 national team caps between them – plus the promise of Fabian Schär from Germany's TSG 1899 Hoffenheim. Lichtsteiner had earned approving reviews from all around Europe when he helped Juventus reach the 2015 UEFA Champions League final, in which they lost to Barcelona.

Gökhan Inler, Valon Behrami and Gelson Fernandes plus the inspiration and goals of Shaqiri delivered similar solidity and consistency in midfield. In attack, Drmic and Seferovic are two more squad-members who play for German clubs, Borussia Mönchengladbach and Eintracht Frankfurt, respectively.

Another measure of Switzerland's

tournament know-how becomes clear when you consider that Djourou, Lichtsteiner, Behrami, Inler and Gelson Fernandes were all members of the Switzerland squad when the country co-hosted the UEFA EURO 2008 finals with Austria. This time, across the border in France, they could benefit from "near-home" advantage.

SWITZERLAND AT THE UEFA EURO FINALS

1960	Did not qualify
1964	Did not qualify
1968	Did not qualify
1972	Did not qualify
1976	Did not qualify
1980	Did not qualify
1984	Did not qualify
1988	Did not qualify
1992	Did not qualify
1996	Group stage
2000	Did not qualify
2004	Group stage
2008	Group stage
2012	Did not qualify

O sa mirë me qenë Shqiptar!
ALBANIA
ALBANIA
O sa mirë me qenë Shqiptar!
ALBANIA
ALBANIA
ALBANIA
ALBANIA
ALBANIA
ALBANIA
ALBANIA
ALBANIA
ALBANIA
ALBANIA
ALBANIA
Përjetësisht!
ALBANIA
ALBANIA
ALBANIA

Albania's supporters have had plenty to cheer about in recent years. Their reward is a place in the 2016 UEFA European Championship, the first major finals the nation will enjoy as participants and not solely spectators.

GROUP B
ENGLAND

At the last European Football Championships, in 2012, England reached the quarter-finals before losing on penalties to Italy. Back then, manager Roy Hodgson had enjoyed only a few weeks in which to prepare his players. This time round, he has had a full four years and expectations will be very different, particularly after the manner in which England qualified for France.

COACH

ROY HODGSON

No manager brought as much high-level tournament experience to the England job as Roy Hodgson when he was rushed into the position ahead of the UEFA EURO 2012 finals following the departure of Fabio Capello. He led his team to the quarter-finals, where they lost on penalties to Italy. Hodgson had previously managed Switzerland at the 1994 FIFA World Cup and UEFA EURO 96. At club level, he also won league titles in Sweden and Denmark and reached UEFA European club finals with Fulham and Internazionale. Hodgson, born in south London on 9 August 1947, led England unbeaten through qualifying for both the 2014 FIFA World Cup and UEFA EURO 2016.

The history of the English game and the worldwide popularity of the Premier League are out of all proportion to the national team's achievements in terms of titles won over the years. They have only won the FIFA World Cup once, 50 years ago – and have never reached the final of the UEFA European Football Championship.

The nearest the Three Lions came was in 1968 when they came third. They also reached the semi-finals as hosts in 1996. The story in recent years, in all major tournaments, has been the same: England have qualified in decisive fashion for the finals, but have then fallen below both their own hopes and their fans' expectations.

Foreign admirers of the Premier League often pose the same question of surprise about the tournament travails of the national team, until they understand that English fans are thrilled every week by a higher percentage of foreign imports than in any other major league. Only recently has the Football Association acted to create more openings for young

BELOW: England were almost perfect in qualifying for UEFA EURO 2016. They won every game, scored the second most goals (31), conceded the second fewest (three) and had the best goal difference (+28).

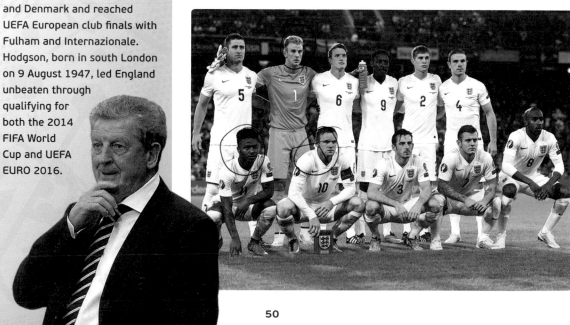

STAR PLAYER
WAYNE ROONEY

POSITION: **Forward** • CLUB: **Manchester United (England)** • AGE: **30**
BORN: **24 October 1985, Liverpool, England**
INTERNATIONAL DEBUT: **12 February 2003, v Australia**
CAPS: **107** • GOALS: **50**

Wayne Rooney made history when, on 8 September 2015, he netted his 50th international goal against Switzerland to pass Sir Bobby Charlton as England's all-time leading goalscorer. Rooney has set records all his career, having become England's youngest-ever debutant at 18 years and four months – a record since beaten by Theo Walcott. England's youngest ever goalscorer, he has played at every major tournament since 2010 and been voted England's Player of the Year on three occasions. At club level, Rooney is second on Manchester United's all-time goal-scoring list, and has won seven major domestic titles as well as the UEFA Champions League and FIFA Club World Cup.

English talent.

Results are not expected overnight but, in the meantime, England manager Roy Hodgson has found an emerging new generation of players to redevelop a team that disappointed at the 2014 FIFA World Cup. England were eliminated after only two games within little more than a week.

Brazil saw the international farewells of long-serving stalwarts such as midfielders Steven Gerrard and Frank Lampard. However, plenty of experience survived into the UEFA EURO 2016 qualifying competition, in the shape of goalkeeper Joe Hart, central defender Gary Cahill, midfielder James Milner and top-scoring new national captain Wayne Rooney.

Central roles in the "new" England side have been offered to Raheem Sterling – another member of the 2014 squad – Tottenham's free-scoring Harry Kane and Everton's creative attacking midfielder Ross Barkley. Injury problems have denied more consistent roles to Liverpool's Jordan Henderson and Daniel Sturridge, as well as to Arsenal's Theo Walcott, Danny Welbeck and Jack Wilshere.

Welbeck scored both goals as England opened their qualifying campaign with a 2–0 win away to Switzerland in Basel. He was on the scoresheet again in the subsequent 5–0 victory over San Marino and England continued in a similar vein, winning every one of their ten matches, scoring 31 goals and conceding only three.

The return victory over San Marino, by 6–0 in Serravalle on 5 September, saw England become the first team to qualify to join hosts France in the finals – with three games still to play.

Rooney opened the scoring from a penalty to equal Sir Bobby Charlton's long-time national record of 49 goals for England. Manchester United's current England hero then made the record his own with goal No.50 next time out against Switzerland. He finished as the group's seven-goal leading scorer.

Hodgson's focus turned then to preparing for the challenge in France and managing expectations about the prospects for his redeveloping team. The England side that beat UEFA EURO 2016 France hosts 2–0 at Wembley last November included six players under the age of 23.

"I do believe we will have the organisation, the discipline and the desire," said Hodgson. "We are young, we are inexperienced and nothing is going to change that. But I'm optimistic, positive and hopeful. This group of players won't let anyone down in terms of their attitude and desire."

ENGLAND AT THE UEFA EURO FINALS

1960	Did not enter
1964	Did not qualify
1968	Third place
1972	Did not qualify
1976	Did not qualify
1980	Group stage
1984	Group stage
1988	Group stage
1992	Did not qualify
1996	Semi-final
2000	Group stage
2004	Quarter-final
2008	Did not qualify
2012	Quarter-final

WALES

Not only will Wales be making their debut in the finals of the UEFA European Football Championship in France, but they will also be stepping out in the finals of a major competition for the first time since they reached the quarter-finals of the FIFA World Cup in 1958 in Sweden. Wales's rise has been spectacular, from a low of 112 in the FIFA World Rankings in October 2010 to No. 8 in October 2015.

COACH

CHRIS COLEMAN

Chris Coleman took over as national team manager of Wales in early 2012 in the most difficult of circumstances following the tragic death of then-manager Gary Speed. Coleman, born on 10 June 1970, played 32 times for Wales between 1992 and 2002 on the back of a successful club career with Manchester City, home-town Swansea, Crystal Palace, Blackburn and Fulham. He was forced to retire as a player after he broke his leg in a car accident in 2001, becoming a coach and manager. He managed Fulham, Real Sociedad in Spain, Coventry City and Larissa in Greece before joining Speed's coaching staff with the Wales national team.

Association football will take centre stage ahead of the rugby code for Wales when Chris Coleman takes his squad to UEFA EURO 2016. Qualification is a vindication for not only Coleman and his players but also for the foundation work undertaken by previous managers John Toshack and Gary Speed, the latter of whom died tragically aged only 46 in 2011.

The present team embodies the resilient spirit demonstrated by the national team ever since the creation of the Football Association of Wales in 1876, the world's third-oldest FA.

The legendary Billy Meredith led Wales to six British Home Championship successes in the inter-war years. New heroes emerged in the 1950s, most notably John Charles – the "Gentle Giant" from Juventus – who led Wales to the last eight at the 1958 FIFA World Cup in Sweden. Other stars of that team included Tottenham wingers Cliff Jones and Terry Medwin, Newcastle inside-left Ivor Allchurch and Arsenal goalkeeper Jack Kelsey.

BELOW: The world's most expensive footballer, Gareth Bale (front row, far left) was Wales's brightest star as they qualified for the UEFA EURO 2016. He scored seven of his country's 11 goals in Group B.

STAR PLAYER
GARETH BALE

POSITION: **Winger** • CLUB: **Real Madrid (Spain)** • AGE: **26**
BORN: **16 July 1989, Cardiff, Wales**
INTERNATIONAL DEBUT: **27 May 2006, v Trinidad & Tobago**
CAPS: **54** • GOALS: **19**

Gareth Bale has set records throughout his career. He was Wales' then-youngest senior international when, as a 16-year-old, he made his debut against Trinidad & Tobago in 2006. Seven years later, he became the world's most expensive player when Real Madrid paid Tottenham €100 million for his services – he went on to win the UEFA Champions League in his first season in Spain. In between, Bale evolved from an attacking left-back into a roaming attacker, notably when he scored a UEFA Champions League hat-trick for Spurs against Internazionale in October 2010. Bale was Wales top scorer with seven goals as they qualified for UEFA EURO 2016, including a dramatic winner at home to Belgium.

Further fine players emerged down the years, such as Liverpool centre-forward Ian Rush and Manchester United's Mark Hughes and Ryan Giggs, but they narrowly failed to reach the finals of the 1994 FIFA World Cup and UEFA EURO 96 – the latter tournament was held just across the border in England.

Hughes took over as manager in the spring of 2000 and again suffered a near miss. Wales reached the qualifying play-offs for UEFA EURO 2004, but lost 1–0 to Russia.

Leading Welsh clubs Cardiff City and Swansea City have been stalwarts in the English league system. Cardiff, famously, became the only club ever to take the FA Cup out of England, thanks to a famous Wembley victory over favourites Arsenal in 1927, while Swansea's passing game has lit up the Premier League since their arrival among English football's elite in 2011.

Their rise coincided with a renewed sense of pride and confidence in Welsh football, with the national team benefiting from a solid core in every department. Former goalkeeper Neville Southall, Wales' record international with 92 caps and a former caretaker

manager, acknowledged the point after the team had secured qualification for France, saying:

"We used to have round pegs in square holes, but we've now got our most balanced squad since 1958, plus a match-winner in Gareth Bale."

Bale and other members of Wales' so-called "golden generation", such as Aaron Ramsey, Joe Ledley, Ashley Williams, Neil Taylor, Joe Allen and Wayne Henessey, were all handed their debuts by Toshack during his managerial stint between 2005 and 2010.

Speed carried on the work by bringing Wales' team preparation into the hi-tech age, and Coleman has built on all of that. Above all, it has been Wales' fortune to boast, in Gareth Bale, one of the most exciting footballers in Europe. Bale, for all the high-pressure club demands at Real Madrid, has remained intensely committed to the Welsh cause.

He scored the two goals that brought Wales victory over Andorra in their opening qualifying tie in September 2014 and then struck the all-important winner at home to group favourites Belgium in

Cardiff the following June. Fittingly, he also wrapped up Wales' run with his seventh goal – joint most in Group B with Bosnia and Herzegovina's Edin Džeko – to seal a 2–0 concluding win over Andorra.

Thus Wales travel to France with every player determined to live up to the motto on their shirts: "Together. Stronger."

WALES AT THE UEFA EURO FINALS

1960	Did not enter
1964	Did not qualify
1968	Did not qualify
1972	Did not qualify
1976	Did not qualify
1980	Did not qualify
1984	Did not qualify
1988	Did not qualify
1992	Did not qualify
1996	Did not qualify
2000	Did not qualify
2004	Did not qualify
2008	Did not qualify
2012	Did not qualify

GROUP B
SLOVAKIA

Although Slovakia have never reached the finals of the UEFA European Football Championship, the manner in which they powered through their qualifying campaign marked them out as dangerous rivals for anyone. And the knowledge that they have already beaten European champions Spain in their preliminary group will provide particular encouragement for Ján Kozák and his men.

COACH

JÁN KOZÁK

Of all the UEFA EURO 2016 coaches, Ján Kozák is one of the most experienced former international players, having scored nine goals in 55 appearances for what was then Czechoslovakia. A former Czechoslovak Player of the Year, Kozák played in midfield at both UEFA EURO 1980 and the 1982 FIFA World Cup. Having won Slovak league titles with FC Košice (in 1997 and 1998) and the domestic cup with MFK Košice (in 2009), he became Slovakia coach in 2013 in succession to Michal Hipp. Now he has made history by becoming the first coach to lead Slovakia to the European finals.

Slovakia is a member of UEFA's "new era club" – the group of countries that emerged into the bright light of independent statehood in the early 1990s. In the case of the Slovaks, this happened after the collapse of the Warsaw Pact, when what was formerly Czechoslovakia was divided into two separate countries – the Czech Republic and Slovakia.

Not that the Slovak region had not played its full part in Czechoslovak success: no fewer than eight members of the team that won the final of the 1976 UEFA European Championship were Slovak. The ŠK Slovan Bratislava club had also earned respect through their regular participation in European club competitions – notably when they won the now-defunct Cup Winners' Cup in 1969.

Slovakia made their international competitive debut in the qualifying tournament for UEFA EURO 1996 and finished third in a tough group

BELOW: Slovakia may have no experience of the UEFA EURO finals as a nation, but the players in their UEFA EURO 2016 squad will be battle-hardened from tough club competition around Europe.

STAR PLAYER
MARTIN ŠKRTEL

POSITION: **Central defender** • CLUB: **Liverpool (England)** • AGE: **31**
BORN: **15 December 1984, Handlová, Slovakia**
INTERNATIONAL DEBUT: **9 July 2004 v Japan**
CAPS: **76** • GOALS: **5**

After earning a reputation for solid defensive work, Martin Škrtel left his first club FK AS Trenčín and moved abroad in the search for trophies. He played initially in Russia with Zenit St Petersburg, with whom he collected the first and to date only league title of his career. A move to Liverpool in 2008 was the ideal preparation for him to play a starring role for Slovakia in their first-ever appearance at a FIFA World Cup finals in 2010, at which they made a surprise run to the second round. Later, back in England, Skrtel won the Football League Cup in 2012 with Liverpool and has established himself as a defensive cornerstone, making more than 300 games for the club.

behind Romania and France. It was a promising start for a new nation still finding its feet in international football, but they had to wait until 2010 – and the FIFA World Cup in South Africa – before they eventually reached the finals stages of a major tournament for the first time.

And they made an impressive debut too, drawing with New Zealand and losing to Paraguay before beating three-times world champions Italy 3–2 to overtake them and secure runners-up slot in the group. Their adventure came to an end in Durban in the second round with a 2–1 defeat by the Netherlands.

However, hopes of building on that achievement foundered when they failed to qualify for both UEFA EURO 2012 and for the 2014 FIFA World Cup finals. That prompted the appointment of Ján Kozák.

The task of qualifying for UEFA EURO 2016 was a challenging one. Slovakia were drawn in a group featuring Spain, as well as an eastern European trio of Ukraine, Belarus and FYR Macedonia. But the Slovaks made a perfect start by winning 1–0 away to Ukraine in Kiev thanks to an early goal from winger Róbert Mak. They followed that up with a 2–1

home victory over reigning European champions Spain. A late goal from "Mino" Stoch secured one of the most important goals in Slovakia's modern football history.

Those two victories provided the solid foundation upon which the Slovaks built to qualify in second place in Group C behind Spain and three points clear of Ukraine – underlining the importance of that initial victory in Kiev in September 2014. Not only that, but attacking midfielder Marek Hamšík, captain and attacking midfielder from Italian club SSC Napoli, wrapped up the campaign as five-goal joint leading marksman in the group along with Spain's Paco Alcácer.

Keeping track of his squad is not an easy task for Kozák and his assistants. Very few of his players are to be found gracing the UEFA Champions League, and many of them are scattered around the Czech Republic, England, Germany, Greece, Italy, Poland, Russia, Scotland and Turkey, as well as in Gulf states such as Qatar and the United Arab Emirates.

However, a significant number of stalwarts in the squad boast

40 international appearances or more. These include defender Peter Pekarík, Ján Ďurica and Martin Škrtel, midfielders Vladimír Weiss, Štanislav Sesták, Hamšík and Stoch, as well as forwards Róbert Vittek and Martin Jakubko.

As a result, Slovakia will boast one of the most experienced of all the squads at UEFA EURO 2016.

SLOVAKIA AT THE UEFA EURO FINALS

1960	Did not exist
1964	Did not exist
1968	Did not exist
1972	Did not exist
1976	Did not exist
1980	Did not exist
1984	Did not exist
1988	Did not exist
1992	Did not exist
1996	Did not qualify
2000	Did not qualify
2004	Did not qualify
2008	Did not qualify
2012	Did not qualify

GROUP B
RUSSIA

Russia confronts a double challenge in France. A positive campaign is vital not only for the sake of national pride but also for the reassurance that comes from a successful UEFA EURO 2016 campaign. Their fans need to know that, after some difficult years, the national team has earned its seat at world football's top table when they host the 2018 FIFA World Cup.

COACH
LEONID SLUTSKY

Born in Volgograd on 4 May 1971, Leonid Slutsky had to retire as a player because of serious injury at the age of 21 and threw his passion for football into coaching. His first major appointment came with local club Olimpia Volgograd in 2000 and he then progressed via Uralan Elista, FC Moscow and PFC Kryila Sovetov Samara to CSKA Moscow, where his seven-year reign brought him league titles in 2013 and 2014, when he was also voted Coach of the Year, as well as the cup in 2013. All this made him a logical candidate to take on a dual role with the national team following Fabio Capello's departure from the position in August 2015. Under his command, Russia duly stepped up from third in the group to an automatic qualification slot.

Russia, in their former guise as the Soviet Union, was the dominant force in the early years of the UEFA European Football Championship – then known as the Nations' Cup.

The USSR won Olympic gold at the 1956 Games in Melbourne and reached the FIFA World Cup quarter-finals on their debut in Sweden in 1958. They went on to triumph in the inaugural continental championship in 1960 with a team that containing some of Soviet football's greatest names, including captain Igor Netto, inside-forward Valentin Ivanov, and the great goalkeeper Lev Yashin.

They defeated Yugoslavia 2–1 in the final in Paris, but this remains the only major national team triumph either the Soviet Union or Russia has celebrated. In that era, the Soviets promised much, but delivered little – losing in the UEFA EURO final in 1964, 1972 and 1988. In between, their best performance at the FIFA World Cup came when they reached the semi-finals in 1966 in England.

BELOW: Russia reached the UEFA EURO semi-final in 2008, but their target at UEFA EURO 2016 is to emulate the old Soviet Union squad of 1960 who were the inaugural champions of the continent.

STAR PLAYER
IGOR AKINFEYEV

POSITION: **Goalkeeper** • CLUB: **CSKA Moscow (Russia)** • AGE: **30**
BORN: **8 April 1986, 1987, Vidnoye-Moscow, Russia**
INTERNATIONAL DEBUT: **28 April 2004 v Norway**
CAPS: **84** • GOALS: **0**

Igor Akinfeyev is one of the few goalkeepers in world football who rank high enough in status to captain their country. He also captains CSKA Moscow, his only senior club, with whom he has won five league titles, six domestic cups, six supercups and, in 2005, the UEFA Cup. He has also won the Lev Yashin Goalkeeper of the Year award on five occasions. He has appeared at three UEFA European Football Championships and at the 2014 FIFA World Cup. Tall and imposing, Akinfeyev made his first competitive appearance for CSKA aged 17 and made his first appearance for the national team a year later when, at 18 years 20 days, he became the youngest international footballer in the history of modern Russia.

In September 1991, the Soviet Union began to disintegrate. Three Baltic states – Estonia, Latvia and Lithuania – achieved independence and went their own way, followed by the other 12 republics. The USSR had qualified for the UEFA EURO 1992 finals, and were allowed to compete as the Commonwealth of Independent States going out in the first round group stage.

The 15 former republics began to organise themselves into new and separate footballing nations. Russia, picking up where the Soviet Union had left off, entered the 1994 FIFA World Cup qualifying competition and qualified for the finals in the United States. There, Oleg Salenko scored a record five goals in a game against Cameroon, but Russia lost the other two games and failed to progress.

Russia have since qualified for the finals of either the FIFA World Cup or the UEFA European Football Championships on seven occasions, but, apart from the semi-finals of UEFA EURO 2008 (where they lost 3–0 to eventual champions Spain), they have failed to advance to the knock-out stages.

Reaching the UEFA EURO 2016 finals in France also proved far from straightforward. Coach Fabio Capello had survived an early exit from the 2014 FIFA World Cup, but he left the post after Russia's first six games in the qualifying campaign produced two wins, two draws and two defeats. It left Russia's players and new coach Leonid Slutsky with much work to do.

Slutsky's competitive debut in September 2015 brought the welcome relief of a 1–0 defeat of Sweden in Moscow. Artem Dzyuba scored the only goal, followed that up with four in a 7–0 win in Liechtenstein and the got the decisive goal in a 2–1 away victory in Moldova. That left Russia needing a victory in the last round at home to Montenegro, which they duly achieved thanks to a 2–0 victory, with goals from Oleg Kuzmin and Aleksandr Kokorin (penalty).

Goalkeeper Igor Akinfeyev has been a pillar of the national team for the past 12 years, one of nine CSKA players summoned by Slutsky. Others, notably, included powerful and experienced defenders Sergei Ignashevich and Aleksei Berezutski, along with mercurial winger Alan Dzagoev, one of the most talented of Russia's emergent generation.

Dzyuba's goal-scoring talents were also welcome and perfectly timed. He finished the qualifying campaign as the group's eight-goal joint top scorer, alongside Sweden's Zlatan Ibrahimović. This is an impressive calling card for UEFA EURO 2016 and his exploits will have been duly noted by the other coaches in Group B.

RUSSIA AT THE UEFA EURO FINALS

1960*	WINNERS
1964*	Runners-up
1968*	Fourth place
1972*	Runners-up
1976*	Did not qualify
1980*	Did not qualify
1984*	Did not qualify
1988*	Runners-up
1992**	Group stage
1996	Group stage
2000	Did not qualify
2004	Group stage
2008	Semi-final
2012	Group stage

* As Soviet Union from 1960–88 and
** Commonwealth of Independent States
in 1992

Football in Wales has reached a new peak in the past half-dozen years, breaking into the world's top 10. Under coach Chris Coleman and led by superstar Gareth Bale (second right) – the world's most expensive footballer – Wales have qualified for their first EURO finals. They did lose to West Germany in the EURO 76 quarter-finals, but then only four nations reached the finals.

GERMANY

In France, Germany will not only be defending their status as world champions, but also their magnificent record in the UEFA European Football Championship. They have been champions and runners-up three times each, and reached the semi-finals twice. However, Germany's last European title came back in 1996 and the 20-year wait is far too long for coach Joachim Löw and his men.

COACH

JOACHIM LÖW

Joachim "Jogi" Löw was Jürgen Klinsmann's assistant when Germany finished third at the 2006 FIFA World Cup finals and went on to succeed him as coach. Löw, born on 3 February 1960, had previously been manager at VfB Stuttgart, Fenerbahçe SK (Turkey), Karlsruher SC, Adanaspor (Turkey), FC Tirol Innsbruck and FK Austria Wien (Austria). He used a blend of technique and physical power to take Germany to the UEFA EURO 2008 final and then introduced a string of talented new youngsters such as Mesut Özil, Thomas Müller and Mario Götze as Germany reached the semi-finals of the FIFA 2010 World Cup. Löw's faith in youth paid dividends: Germany reached the last four at UEFA EURO 2012 too before going on to lift the ultimate prize at the 2014 FIFA World Cup.

Germany attacked the UEFA EURO 2016 qualifying tournament aware that their triumph at the FIFA World Cup in Brazil in July 2014 would serve only to inspire all their opponents in Group D. The opportunity to take the scalp of the world champions would provide an extra incentive for Poland, Ireland, Scotland and Georgia, while Gibraltar would simply have been thrilled to be playing on the UEFA competitive stage for the first time.

Not that Germany are unused to target status: their record of success since the Second World War is unparalleled in the European game. The pre-war era had brought "only" a third-place finish at the 1934 FIFA World Cup, but the game flourished in West Germany – the German Federal Republic – in the post-war era.

Excluded from FIFA in 1946, they were readmitted to the world game in 1950 and won the FIFA World Cup four years later. That victory, engineered by coach Sepp

BELOW: Winners of the FIFA World Cup in 2014, Germany, with a core of players from Bayern Munich – one of Europe's strongest clubs – will be a team all their rivals will fear at UEFA EURO 2016.

STAR PLAYER
THOMAS MÜLLER

POSITION: **Striker** · CLUB: **Bayern Munich (Germany)** · AGE: **26**
BORN: **13 September 1989**
INTERNATIONAL DEBUT: **3 March 2010 v Argentina**
CAPS: **67** · GOALS: **31**

Thomas Müller is the latest "Müller" from Germany to intimidate opponents with his brilliance in and around the penalty box. A product of Bayern's academy, he crowned a magical first season in senior football in 2009–10 by sharing in a league and cup double and then winning both the Golden Boot (with five goals) and Best Young Player awards at the 2010 FIFA World Cup finals in South Africa – at which Germany reached the semi-finals. Four years later, he was Germany's five-goal second-top scorer as they won the FIFA World Cup. At club level, Müller's attacking prowess has brought him four Bundesliga titles, three German cups and, in 2013, the UEFA Champions League and FIFA Club World Cup.

Herberger, was all the more amazing because their opponents in the final were the "Magic Magyars", whose 3–2 defeat was only their second loss in five years.

From then on the Germans grew in stature. At the FIFA World Cup, they were semi-finalists in 1958, quarter-finalists in 1962 and runners-up in 1966.

The 1970s seemed to belong to Bayern Munich and West Germany. Bayern won a hat-trick of European Cups in 1974, 1975 and 1976 and provided the nucleus of the national side that won the UEFA European Football Championship in 1972, the FIFA World Cup in 1974 and, after finishing second in 1976, the European title once again in 1980.

Franz Beckenbauer revolutionised the sweeper's role into one of attack as well as defence while Gerd Müller was a goal-scoring machine with 68 goals in 62 internationals. Later heroes included Karl-Heinz Rummenigge, Lothar Matthäus, Rudi Völler, Jürgen Klinsmann, Thomas Hässler and Matthias Sammer.

Following the FIFA World Cup success and German reunification in 1990, the Germans capitalised on their new-found resources by

securing victory at UEFA EURO 96. That was their last senior title, until their dramatic victory in the final of the 2014 FIFA World Cup against Argentina, thanks to a goal, late in the second period of extra-time, from substitute Mario Götze.

For coach Joachim Löw, however, the new challenge presented by UEFA EURO 2016 required a new team, particularly following the retirement of so many of the 2014 FIFA World Cup winners. Two goals from Thomas Müller secured a narrow 2–1 win over Scotland, but next came a 2–0 defeat in Poland and then a 1–1 home draw with the Republic of Ireland.

Three victories over Gibraltar (twice) and Georgia brought Germany back on track, and a 3–1 home win over Poland fired them to the top of the table, a status they maintained all the way to the end of the qualifying competition, despite losing 1–0 to the Republic of Ireland in Dublin in the penultimate round of matches.

Only one man played all 900 minutes in the ten qualifying ties, Bayern defender Jérôme Boateng, closely followed by club-mate Manuel Neuer, probably the world's

best goalkeeper. Other pillars of the team were Borussia Dortmund's central defender Mats Hummel, Real Madrid midfielder Toni Kroos and the Bayern attacking pair of Müller and Götze.

Müller was Germany's nine-goal top scorer in the qualifying campaign and he is sure to be as dangerous as ever in the finals.

GERMANY AT THE UEFA EURO FINALS

1960*	Did not enter
1964*	Did not enter
1968*	Did not qualify
1972*	WINNERS
1976*	Runners-up
1980*	WINNERS
1984*	Group stage
1988*	Semi-final
1992	Runners-up
1996	WINNERS
2000	Group stage
2004	Group stage
2008	Runners-up
2012	Semi-final

* As West Germany from 1960-88

GROUP C
POLAND

Polish fans believe that the "new" national team being fired in attack by the prolific Robert Lewandowski has the potential to go on and rival the standard set by the great team of the 1970s. Even that team, however, were unable to make a major impact upon the UEFA European Football Championship, and so coach Adam Nawalka and his men have everything to gain in France.

COACH
ADAM NAWAŁKA

Adam Nawałka was an excellent midfielder in the Poland team that reached the second-round group stage of the 1978 FIFA World Cup in Argentina. He spent his entire senior club career with home town Wisła Kraków, the club at which he also began his top-level coaching career. Poland's failure to reach the 2014 FIFA World Cup finals led to him succeeding Waldemar Fornalik as national coach. At that point, Nawałka, born on 23 October 1957, had not won a title or cup as a club coach. However, his credibility as national coach was assured after Poland opened the home programme of the UEFA EURO 2016 qualifying competition with a 2–0 win over world champions Germany.

Poland's football history has been a turbulent one, partly because of the weight of the historical events inflicted on a state that was only created in 1921 – the same year the national team made their international football debut, against Hungary.

Despite reaching the 1938 FIFA World Cup finals, Poland's pre-war record was poor, but the post-war Communist take-over brought great change. Clubs became attached to government bodies and new ones were formed – notably Górnik Zabrze, who reached the UEFA European Cup Winners' Cup final in 1969.

Immediately afterwards, Poland's national team embarked on a 15-year run of achievement, sparked by their gold-medal glory in the football competition at the 1972 Olympic Games in Munich. Their fine young team boasted outstanding individuals, such as Górnik forward Wlodzimierz Lubański, playmaker Kazimierz Deyna and astute left winger Robert Gadocha.

This trio was joined at the 1974 FIFA World Cup finals by Gregorz

BELOW: Poland will be keen to improve on their record in the UEFA European Championship, having reached the finals only twice and failed to advance beyond the group stage on either occasion.

STAR PLAYER
ROBERT LEWANDOWSKI

POSITION: **Centre-forward** • CLUB: **FC Bayern Munich (Germany)** •
AGE: **27** • BORN: **21 August 1988, Warsaw, Poland**
INTERNATIONAL DEBUT: **10 September 2008 v San Marino**
CAPS: **72** • GOALS: **32**

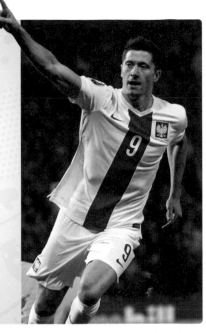

Robert Lewandowski's prolific goal-scoring achievements have already, at 27, earned him a ranking equal to Polish attacking heroes of yesteryear such as Ernest Pol, Wlodzimierz Lubański and Grzegorz Lato. After being league top scorer in Poland with KKS Lech Poznán, he moved to Germany and became the fastest-scoring foreign player to reach 100 goals with his feats for Borussia Dortmund and FC Bayern. He set a European club record when netting five goals in nine minutes for Bayern against Wolfsburg in the 2014–15 season. Already the fifth leading scorer in Poland's history – with 32 goals in 72 appearances – he led his country's attack at both UEFA EURO 2012 and the 2014 FIFA World Cup.

Lato, Poland's second most capped player (100 times), with Jan Tomaszewski in goal. Poland finished third with a team that stayed together for most of the decade and reached the FIFA World Cup finals again in 1978.

More success followed at the 1982 finals, when, with Zbigniew Boniek outstanding, Poland reached the semi-finals. They also reached the second round in 1986, but then the collapse of Communism in the early 1990s led to the withdrawal of state subsidies and the clubs were forced to sell their star players. The national team suffered as a result.

Sixteen years would pass before they returned to the FIFA World Cup finals, and they did not reach the final stages of the UEFA European Football Championship until 2008. Perhaps overawed, they finished fourth in a difficult group that featured Croatia, Germany and co-hosts Austria.

Four years later, Poland were the centre of attention at the finals when they co-hosted the tournament with neighbouring Ukraine. Coach Franciszek Smuda opted for a blend of youth and experience, but again they finished fourth in their group and failed to progress. They had,

however, discovered a centre-forward in Robert Lewandowski, whose goal-scoring feats would soon generate headlines around the world.

Not the least of Lewandowski's achievements came when he scored four times as Poland opened their UEFA EURO 2016 qualifying account with a 7–0 victory over newcomers Gibraltar in a match played in the Algarve, Portugal. New coach Adam Nawałka's team followed up with a proud 2–0 win over Germany, and Lewandowski went on to claim a second hat-trick of the competition against Georgia.

Poland were by no means a one-man team, however. Premier League rivals Wojciech Szczęsny, Lukasz Fabianski and Artur Boruc competed for the goalkeeping berth behind lively Lukasz Piszczek and a midfield springboard featuring versatile Maciej Rybus along with Grzegorz Krychowiak and Arkadiusz Milik from Ajax.

As a result, it was hardly a surprise when Poland ended the campaign assured of a place in France as runners-up to Germany. Lewandowski was leading marksman in the entire qualifying competition with 13

goals, Milik contributed six and Kamil Grosicki four.

Poland, with 33 goals to their credit, were top scorers in all the eight groups, ahead of England (31), Belgium and Germany (24) and Spain (23) – an impressive statistic which surely will have caught the attention of everyone at the finals in France.

POLAND AT THE UEFA EURO FINALS

1960	Did not qualify
1964	Did not qualify
1968	Did not qualify
1972	Did not qualify
1976	Did not qualify
1980	Did not qualify
1984	Did not qualify
1988	Did not qualify
1992	Did not qualify
1996	Did not qualify
2000	Did not qualify
2004	Did not qualify
2008	Group stage
2012	Group stage

UKRAINE

Ukraine laid to rest their play-off jinx in reaching UEFA EURO 2016. Andriy Yarmolenko, their four-goal top scorer in qualifying, struck twice again in their play-off victory over Slovenia and will carry the weight of expectation on only Ukraine's second appearance at the UEFA EURO finals.

COACH

MYKHAILO FOMENKO

Mykhailo Fomenko was a key member of the outstanding Dynamo Kyiv team of the 1970s that, in 1975, enjoyed success in both the UEFA Cup Winners' Cup and the UEFA Super Cup. He played more than 200 matches over seven years with the club and won 24 caps for the Soviet national team. In 1980, after retiring, he joined the Kyiv coaching staff and subsequently moved between more than a dozen appointments, including in Iraq and Guinea, before being handed the Ukraine job in December 2012 in succession to Oleh Blokhin. Ukraine narrowly missed out on a place at the 2014 FIFA World Cup finals after losing a play-off to France, but made no mistake in the UEFA EURO 2016 play-off against Slovenia.

Ukraine's presence in France will provide the country with a pleasant distraction after the travails it has endured since it was a proud and warm co-host at the 2012 tournament. The national team failed, narrowly, to progress beyond the group stage, but that did not prevent local fans from supporting the tournament right through to the final whistle of Spain's crowning victory over Italy.

Under the circumstances – the national championship in the east of the country has been hugely disrupted by the ongoing conflict – the national team's success in qualifying for the finals, for the first time (as co-hosts they qualified automatically four years ago), was a remarkable achievement.

Ukraine has always been a fervent football nation, back to the days of the Soviet Union. In the 1970s and much of the 1980s, the stars of Dynamo Kyiv provided a foundation for the Soviet national team, while the club itself won the UEFA Cup Winners' Cup twice (in 1975 and 1986). Players such Anatoliy Byshovets then Oleh Blokhin, Viktor Kolotov and Volodymyr Onyshchenko were admired across Europe for their skill and style.

BELOW: Ukraine qualified for UEFA EURO 2016 through the playoffs, beating Slovenia 3–1 on aggregate, and now their target is to advance to the knock-out stages.

STAR PLAYER
ANATOLIY TYMOSHCHUK

POSITION: **Midfield** · CLUB: **FC Kairat (Kazakhstan)** · AGE: **37**
BORN: **30 March 1979, Lutsk, Ukraine**
INTERNATIONAL DEBUT: **26 April 2000, v Bulgaria**
CAPS: **140** · GOALS: **4**

Anatoliy Tymoshchuk will crown a remarkable career by captaining his country at UEFA EURO 2016. Tymoshchuk was a teenage ballboy with local side FC Volyn Lutsk when he began his career and was converted from a striker to a midfielder by FC Shakhtar Donetsk. He won three league titles before moving to Russia's Zenit St Petersburg with whom he lifted, as captain, the UEFA Cup and Super Cup (in 2007–08). In 2009, he moved to Bayern Munich with whom he won the UEFA Champions League as well as German league and cup, while establishing himself as Ukraine's record international. In 2011, Tymoshchuk was nominated as the greatest player in his country's history.

Considering the strengths of not only Dynamo Kyiv but also Shakhtar Donetsk, it was a surprise that Ukraine's national team took time to "take off" following independence in the early 1990s after the fragmentation of the Soviet Union.

Ukraine's first finals was the FIFA World Cup in 2006 – they made the quarter-finals – and their next major tournament finals was UEFA EURO 2012. Despite the efforts of long-time hero Andriy Shevchenko, they finished behind England and France in their group and were eliminated.

Blokhin, who had coached Ukraine at the finals, stood down following the tournament and succeeded in quick, caretaker succession by former Dynamo Kyiv team-mates Andriy Bal, Oleksandr Zavarov and, finally, Mykhailo Fomenko. Zavarov and Onyshchenko now feature among Fomenko's coaching staff.

Conveniently for Fomenko, the vast majority of his squad play their club football in Ukraine. Two notable exceptions are veteran captain and anchor man Anatoliy Tymoshchuk, who plays in Kazakhstan, and flying forward Yevhen Konoplyanka, who plies his trade with Spain's double UEFA Cup winners Sevilla FC.

Konoplyanka, voted Ukraine's Footballer of the Year on three occasions, brings the experience he has gained at club level with both Dnipro Dnipropetrovsk and Sevilla, both in the UEFA Champions League and the UEFA Europa League, to the national team. The team wants to avoid repeating the painful lessons they suffered at UEFA EURO 2012 and the defeat by France in the 2014 FIFA World Cup qualifying play-offs.

An experienced supporting cast provides a solid pillar throughout Ukraine's team. In defence, they have Shakhtar goalkeeper Andriy Pyatov and his club-mates Vyacheslav Shevchuk, Oleksandr Kucher and Yaroslav Rakitskyi.

A versatility to defend, work and launch high-speed counter-attacks are the hallmarks of a midfield in which Tymoshchuk and Konoplyanka are supported by Dynamo's experienced Oleh Husyev and Andriy Yarmolenko.

Defensively Ukraine were one of the most solid in qualifying with only four goals conceded, but their biggest challenge is scoring goals – they managed only 14 in ten Group C matches. They finished behind Spain and Slovakia, losing their

opening match 1–0 at home to the Slovaks and lost twice to Spain.

In the playoff against Slovenia, however, Ukraine rose to the occasion. At home, in Lviv, a goal in each half from Yarmolenko and Yevhen Seleznyov provided a 2–0 cushion. A late Yarmolenko strike then secured a 1–1 draw in Maribor. Ukraine, at last, had broken their play-off jinx.

UKRAINE AT THE UEFA EURO FINALS

1960	Did not exist
1964	Did not exist
1968	Did not exist
1972	Did not exist
1976	Did not exist
1980	Did not exist
1984	Did not exist
1988	Did not exist
1992	Did not exist
1996	Did not qualify
2000	Did not qualify
2004	Did not qualify
2008	Did not qualify
2012	Group stage

NORTHERN IRELAND

As a player, Michael O'Neill made 31 international appearances for Northern Ireland; but it is as the country's manager that he achieved an even more outstanding feat than anything he did on the pitch. Northern Ireland's appearance at UEFA EURO 2016 will be the first time they have mixed with football's elite since the 1986 FIFA World Cup.

COACH

MICHAEL O'NEILL

Michael O'Neill applied all the football know-how he had gained in virtually every corner of British and Irish football to bring Northern Ireland to the UEFA EURO finals for the first time. O'Neill was born in Portadown, Northern Ireland, on 5 July 1969, and played club football in England, Scotland and the United States, while winning 31 international caps. After working briefly in financial services, he took up football management and, in 2011–12, his Shamrock Rovers team became the first League of Ireland club to reach the group stages of a European competition (the UEFA Europa League). He became Northern Ireland manager in December 2011, succeeding Nigel Worthington.

After a 30-year absence from an international tournament finals, the team from the world's fourth-oldest football association, Northern Ireland is back among the game's elite.

The achievement of Michael O'Neill's team in reaching UEFA EURO 2016 has provided both a welcome reward and encouragement for football in Ulster, whose singular identity has been forged proudly through 136 years of international football. The Irish Football Association was founded in November 1880 and, between 1881 and 1921, Ireland was represented by one national team.

Then, in 1921, the jurisdiction of the Irish Football Association was reduced solely to Northern Ireland, after the secession of clubs in the soon-to-be Irish Free State – although its team remained the national team for all of Ireland until 1950 and used the name Ireland until the 1970s.

It was not until 1951, when France visited Belfast, that non-British sides were engaged. Northern Ireland then qualified for the 1958 FIFA World Cup finals, led by Tottenham's Danny Blanchflower, and fared better than England and Scotland in reaching the quarter-finals.

BELOW: Northern Ireland have played in three FIFA World Cup finals (and reached the quarter-finals in 1958 and 1982), but UEFA EURO 2016 is their UEFA European Football Championship finals debut.

STAR PLAYER
STEVEN DAVIS

POSITION: **Midfielder** · CLUB: **Southampton (England)** · AGE: **31**
BORN: **1 January 1985, Ballymena, Northern Ireland**
INTERNATIONAL DEBUT: **9 February 2005, v Canada**
CAPS: **78** · GOALS: **7**

Steven Davis, Northern Ireland's supremely consistent midfielder, has reached a remarkable career pinnacle. Not only is he poised to captain his country in their first-ever appearance at the UEFA EURO finals, but he has also emerged as a key member of a Southampton side whose style has lit up the English Premier League. Davis made his league debut with Aston Villa in 2004 and went on to win various fans' awards before being sold to Fulham in 2007 and then moved on loan to Scotland's Rangers. He shared in Rangers' progress to the 2008 UEFA Cup final and triumphs in the Scottish league, league cup and SFA Cup. Rangers' financial collapse set him free to return to English football with Southampton in 2012.

In the 1960s and 1970s, despite the presence of George Best in the team, Northern Irish football was at a low ebb, but they revived in the 1980s. Managed by Billy Bingham, who had played for the side in 1958, Northern Ireland reached the second round of the 1982 FIFA World Cup, and qualified again in 1986. Pat Jennings, one of the all-time greatest British goalkeepers, was the star of that side.

His retirement in 1986 led to years of disappointment. A revival of sorts started in 2004, when, under the management of Lawrie Sanchez, Northern Ireland ended a run of 16 games without a win. Gradually the revival picked up speed. In 2005, Northern Ireland beat England 1–0 in a FIFA World Cup qualifier and, 12 months later, they scored a famous 3–2 victory over Spain in a UEFA EURO 2008 qualifying group tie.

Still, though, a place in the finals eluded them. The managerial baton then passed from Sanchez to Nigel Worthington and then on to O'Neill. Qualification for the 2014 FIFA World Cup finals proved too testing for a revamped team, but O'Neill's work bore fruit when Northern Ireland qualified for their first ever European finals by defeating Greece

3–1 at Windsor Park in Belfast in October 2015.

The size of Northern Ireland's achievement can be seen in the fact that the squad leans heavily on English lower division clubs, with only a handful of players coming from the Premier League. Chief among them were West Bromwich Albion defenders Jonny Evans and Gareth McAuley and their midfielder Chris Brunt, skipper Steven Davis from Southampton and the powerful Kyle Lafferty, from Norwich, in attack.

Lafferty is one of O'Neill's most internationally experienced players. He began his career Burnley and then went on to win six trophies with Rangers in Scotland. He then played for FC Sion in Switzerland and Palermo in Italy before returning to the English game with Norwich. With 16 goals he now ranks second as Northern Ireland's all-time highest scorer behind David Healy (36).

Lafferty and his team-mates did not "merely" qualify for France. They finished top of qualifying Group F, one point ahead of Romania. They also finished five points clear of third-placed Hungary. That status underlined the importance of their

campaign-opening 2–1 victory over the Hungarians in Budapest.

Lafferty scored the winner two minutes from the end and went on to finish as the group's seven-goal leading marksman. They lost only one of their ten games en route to France. As the traditional song says: "Irish eyes were (very definitely) smiling."

NORTHERN IRELAND AT THE UEFA EURO FINALS

1960	Did not enter
1964	Did not qualify
1968	Did not qualify
1972	Did not qualify
1976	Did not qualify
1980	Did not qualify
1984	Did not qualify
1988	Did not qualify
1992	Did not qualify
1996	Did not qualify
2000	Did not qualify
2004	Did not qualify
2008	Did not qualify
2012	Did not qualify

Northern Ireland produced their most consistent qualifying competition run for almost 30 years as they emerged as winners of UEFA EURO 2016 Qualifying Group F, ahead of Romania and Hungary. A decade ago, they beat England (FIFA World Cup 2006) and Spain (UEFA EURO 2008) in qualifying matches, but did not even reach the play-offs.

GROUP D
SPAIN

After relinquishing their FIFA World Cup crown in Brazil in 2014, Spain's focus turns to the UEFA EURO 2016 finals as they look to become the competition's first four-time winners. A fine crop of new young players has emerged to ease coach Vicente del Bosque's task in developing a team that is a worthy successor to the one that became European champions in 2008 and 2012.

COACH

VICENTE DEL BOSQUE

Vicente del Bosque, born on 23 December 1950, is one of only two managers (Germany's Helmut Schön is the other) to have led his nation to both world and European crowns – in 2010 and 2012 respectively in the case of del Bosque. The former Spain midfielder first turned down an approach to lead Spain after Euro 2004, but he changed his mind four years later and succeeded Luis Aragonés as coach after Spain's victorious UEFA EURO 2008 campaign. Spain won their first ten games under del Bosque, breaking the previous international record of nine (by Brazil in 1969), and went on to win the 2010 FIFA World Cup and UEFA EURO 2012 under his low-key leadership.

At one time, Spain's reputation as a world football power was based almost exclusively on the exploits of its world-famous clubs, particularly Real Madrid CF and FC Barcelona. Then the national team embarked on a sensational run of three major tournament triumphs between 2008 and 2012 to confirm Spain as the great power of world football.

Football first gained a foothold in the Basque region of northern Spain in the 1890s, thanks to migrant British workers. Indeed, Spain's oldest club, Athletic Bilbao, still retains its English title. The game spread rapidly, and was soon popular in Madrid,

Barcelona and Valencia.

The Real Federacion Española de Futbol was founded in 1913 and the national team made their debut at the 1928 Olympic Games in Antwerp. They reached the quarter-finals on that occasion and again at the 1934 FIFA World Cup, with a team starring legendary goalkeeper Ricardo Zamora.

Madrid and Barcelona, the Clasico rivals, provided glamour and glory to the early years of European club competition in the 1950s, largely on the back of imported talent. Madrid boasted Argentina's Alfredo Di Stefano and Hungarian Ferenc Puskás, while

BELOW: Until Spain achieved it in 2012, no country had successfully defended their UEFA EURO title, so now their target is to become the first team to win three consecutive tournaments.

STAR PLAYER
ANDRÉS INIESTA

POSITION: **Midfielder** • CLUB: **Barcelona (Spain)** • AGE: **29**
BORN: **11 May 1984, Fuentealbilla, Spain**
INTERNATIONAL DEBUT: **27 May 2006, v Russia**
CAPS: **106** • GOALS: **13**

Andrés Iniesta ranks among the greatest Spanish footballers of all time. He has played for his country at every level and has won 25 titles with Barcelona (including the UEFA Champions League four times) and was part of the Spain side that won the UEFA European Football Championship in 2008 and 2012, either side of the FIFA World Cup in 2010. His midfield partnership with Xavi Hernández made Barcelona almost untouchable between 2006 and 2015, and wrote a personal page in football history when he scored the winning goal against the Netherlands in the 2010 FIFA World Cup final. His Spain team-mate Fernando Torres once said of him: "I have never seen him play a bad game."

Barça had their own Hungarian trio of László Kubala, Sándor Kocsis and Zoltán Czibor.

But new Spanish heroes were evolving. Barcelona schemer Luis Suárez and Madrid winger Amancio were key members of the Spain side who, as hosts, won the European crown for the first time in 1964. They defeated defending champions the Soviet Union 2–1 in Madrid's Estadio Bernabeu to clinch Spain's first major international trophy.

The national team went into decline for two decades until a revival brought quarter-finals progress at the 1986 FIFA World Cup in Mexico.

Six years later, Spain's youngsters won Olympic gold in Barcelona with a team including Pep Guardiola who, as player and then coach, would go on to play a key role in revitalising the national team. The work of ex-Real Madrid wing half Juan Santisteban with the youth teams was equally important.

Spain's seniors reached the quarter-finals of both the 1994 FIFA World Cup and UEFA EURO 96 and then went on to command the world and European game in the 21st century. Spain beat Germany 1–0 at UEFA EURO 2008,

the Netherlands by the same margin at the 2010 FIFA World Cup and then Italy 4–0 at UEFA EURO 2012.

Del Bosque benefits from competition for places all over his team. Veteran goalkeeper and captain Iker Casillas, with more than 160 caps, has been pushed by David De Gea behind a defence in which Real Madrid's Sergio Ramos and Barcelona's Gerard Piqué put aside their club rivalries in the national interest.

In midfield, Andrés Iniesta and Sergio Busquets remain permanent fixtures, while the retirement of Xavi Hernández from international football has opened up opportunities for Premier League-based David Silva, Juan Mata and Santi Cazorla.

Other exports in the shape of Chelsea's Diego Costa and Juventus' Álvaro Morata joust to lead the attack. They face competition from Valencia's Paco Alcácer, who was Spain's top scorer in qualifying with five goals.

Not surprisingly, Spain had few problems securing their place at the UEFA EURO 2016 finals. They began their Group C campaign in style with a 5–1 victory over FYR Macedonia and went on to win nine of their

ten games, scoring 23 goals and conceding a mere three (equal with England as the best defence).

A lone defeat, by 2–1 away to Slovakia, was Spain's first qualifying defeat since October 2006, but they still ended the group five points clear of runners-up Slovakia and look like ominously dangerous title contenders once more.

SPAIN AT THE UEFA EURO FINALS

1960	Withdrew
1964	WINNERS
1968	Did not qualify
1972	Did not qualify
1976	Did not qualify
1980	Group stage
1984	Runners-up
1988	Group stage
1992	Did not qualify
1996	Quarter-final
2000	Quarter-final
2004	Group stage
2008	WINNERS
2012	WINNERS

GROUP D
CZECH REPUBLIC

The Czechs have been a central force in European football for the past century, whatever the politically drawn borders may have been. On this occasion, coach Pavel Vrba will bring to France and UEFA EURO 2016 a team representing a nation that can look back with pride on the victory it achieved in 1976 and a presence at the finals for every one of the past five tournaments.

COACH

PAVEL VRBA

Pavel Vrba took over as manager of Czech Republic early in 2014 after, in his own words, "five wonderful years" with Viktoria Plzen whom he led to two league titles and one cup. He had previously won the Slovak title with Zilina. His predecessor as Czech coach, Josef Pesice, had stepped down after the team failed to reach the 2014 FIFA World Cup finals in Brazil. Vrba was set the target of putting that right by qualifying for UEFA EURO 2016 – a feat his team achieved with a game to spare. Vrba's coaching hero was Karel Bruckner, who led the Czechs to the semi-finals at UEFA EURO 2004 in Portugal. Vrba had previously turned down an offer to manage neighbours Slovakia.

Following the disappointment of failing to reach the 2014 FIFA World Cup finals, the Czech Republic have bounced back impressively by qualifying for UEFA EURO 2016 with a rebuilt team. Bořek Dočkhal, their four-goal leading scorer in the qualifying campaign, proved an ideal representative of a new generation of players who have gained a broad experience both at home and abroad.

Czech football began long before Czechoslovakia had even been founded, in the years before the First World War, when the Hapsburg empire dominated central Europe. The game was launched separately in both what was then Bohemia and in Slovakia.

Sports clubs had been created on a German-inspired model and, in the 1880s, Slavia of Prague were the first to add football to their curriculum. However, it was traditional rivals Sparta who won the first Bohemia championship in 1912 before the onset of the First World War – the climax of which led to the creation of a new national identity.

The football federation of the fledgling Czecho-Slovakia (as it was originally styled) was one of the first not merely to accept but to welcome professionalism.

BELOW: The Czech Republic qualified for UEFA EURO 2016 in some style, winning Group A, and this squad will be looking to go one better than the class of 1996, when they lost in the final at Wembley.

STAR PLAYER
PETR ČECH

POSITION: **Goalkeeper** • CLUB: **Arsenal (England)** • AGE: **34**
BORN: **20 May 1982, Plzen, Czech Republic**
INTERNATIONAL DEBUT: **12 February 2002 v Hungary**
CAPS: **117** • GOALS: **0**

Petr Čech has been one of the finest goalkeepers in the world for more than a decade, having accelerated up the club ladder with Chmel Blašny and AC Sparta Praha (in the Czech Republic), Stade Rennais FC (France), and both Chelsea and Arsenal in England. His honours list include the UEFA Champions League in 2012, the UEFA Europa League a year later and four Premier League titles, four FA Cups and three League Cups (all with Chelsea). Of the more than 20 personal awards he has received over the years, seven were Czech Republic Footballer of the Year. Čech's trademark has become the protective, rugby-style headgear he wears on the field – he first used it after suffering a serious head injury in 2006.

As a result, the Czechs were among Europe's leading football nations throughout the inter-war years. Sparta and Slavia dominated the Mitropa Cup – forerunner of the modern-day European club tournaments – and the national team finished runners-up to hosts Italy at the 1934 FIFA World Cup. Goalkeeper Frantisek Planicka and forwards Oldrich Nejedly and Antonin Puc were the great heroes of their day.

After the Second World War and the communist takeover of the country, army club Dukla, with a great left-back in Ladislav Novak and two wonderful, complementary wing-halves in Svatopluk Pluskal and Josef Masopust, provided the foundation for a national team that regularly reached the FIFA World Cup finals and which finished as runners-up to Brazil in 1962.

Czechoslovakia were also among the powerful early contenders in the UEFA European Football Championship, winning a thrilling final in 1976 and finishing third in 1980. Each time they owned their status to penalties, edging West Germany in a shoot-out in 1976 – with Antonin Panenka's legendary spot kick – and then Italy in the third-place match in Naples in 1980.

A quarter-final appearance at the 1990 FIFA World Cup, again in Italy, proved an international swansong, however, before the split between the Czechs and the Slovaks. Now appearing as the Czech Republic, they finished as runners-up at UEFA EURO 96 in England, losing only on the golden-goal rule to Germany in the final. The Czechs have been ever-presents at the finals ever since. It proved the Czechs had suffered little from the football separation.

Heroes of this new era were winger Karel Poborský and midfielders Patrik Berger and Radek Bejbl.

Coach Pavel Vrba took over the role of coach following the team's failure to qualify for the 2014 FIFA World Cup and was determined to rebuild a team by mixing the experience of foreign-based stars with new talents emerging from the youth sector.

The most dangerous rivals before the launch of Group A qualifying action were considered to be the Netherlands, who had just finished third in Brazil – but a 2–1 victory in Prague, secured by a stoppage-time winner from Václav Pilař, provided a perfect springboard.

The Czechs lost only two of their ten games and were assured of their place in the finals with two rounds of matches to spare. A 2–1 away victory over Latvia following first-half strikes from David Limberský and Vladimír Darida meant Vrba had completed the first half of his mission.

Now for the second half – in France.

CZECH REPUBLIC AT THE UEFA EURO FINALS

1960*	Third place
1964*	Did not qualify
1968*	Did not qualify
1972*	Did not qualify
1976*	WINNERS
1980*	Third place
1984*	Did not qualify
1988*	Did not qualify
1992*	Did not qualify
1996	Runners-up
2000	Group stage
2004	Semi-final
2008	Group stage
2012	Quarter-final

* As Czechoslovakia from 1960–92

GROUP D
TURKEY

Turkey are back in the UEFA European Football Championship finals for only the fourth time in their history. Coach Fatih Terim led them to the semi-finals in Austria and Switzerland on their last appearance in the tournament in 2008, setting his new team a high standard to emulate. Their stars play at Europe's top clubs, so they have the quality and experience to succeed at UEFA EURO 2016.

COACH
FATIH TERIM

Fatih Terim, nicknamed "The Emperor", is now in his third spell as Turkey manager. Born on 4 September 1953, Terim played 51 times for his country between 1975 and 1985 and was a favourite in central defence for Galatasaray. His coaching CV includes spells in Italy with Fiorentina and Milan. Terim made an imposing start to his first stint as national coach by taking Turkey to the finals of UEFA EURO 96. He returned in 2005 and led them to the semi-finals of UEFA EURO 2008, in which they lost to Germany. It remains Turkey's best-ever showing at an international tournament. He was reappointed in August 2013 in place of Abdullah Avci.

Once upon a time Turkish football was an also-ran on the European stage. The national team never reached the big tournaments and could not cope with away-game pressures, and the clubs had plenty of domestic history but little else.

Then, over two decades, everything changed. Now there are no longer any "easy" matches against Turkish teams, while clubs such as Galatasaray AŞ and Fenerbahçe SK – situated on opposite sides of the Bosphorus – boast magnificent training complexes and passionate support.

Turkey's first club, Black Stocking, was formed at the turn of the century after English traders brought the game to the Ottoman Empire. A Turkish football federation was founded in 1923, months before the creation of the Turkish Republic. The national team's first taste of foreign competition came a year later, at the Olympic Games in Paris – they lost 5–2 in the first round to Czechoslovakia.

BELOW: Turkey were the first country to automatically go through to the UEFA EURO finals from third place in the qualifying group. They had the best record of the nine third-place teams in their groups.

STAR PLAYER
ARDA TURAN

POSITION: **Winger/midfielder** • CLUB: **Barcelona (Spain)** • AGE: **29**
BORN: **30 January 1987, Fatih, Turkey**
INTERNATIONAL DEBUT: **16 August 2006, v Luxembourg**
CAPS: **83** • GOALS: **15**

Arda Turan is one of the finest Turkish football exports for many years. His pace, skill and direct style quickly made him a favourite as a teenager with Istanbul club Galatasaray AŞ. Promoted to the senior squad by coach Gheorghe Hagi, Turan won the Turkish league and cup and was soon appointed club captain. In 2011, he became the most expensive Turkish export ever when Atlético de Madrid signed him for €12 million. With them he went on to win further league and cup honours, including the UEFA Europa League and the UEFA Super Cup before moving on to Barcelona in July 2015. He has been voted Turkey's footballer of the year on three occasions, as well as the country's sportsman of the year.

Turkey won a place at the 1950 FIFA World Cup finals after beating Syria 7–0, but were unable to attend the tournament in Brazil because of a lack of funds. They qualified again in 1954, but fell in the first round.

The launch of a full national championship in 1960 helped Turkey make up for lost time. Experienced coaches such as Brian Birch, Don Howe, Malcolm Allison and Gordon Milne (from England), Sebastiao Lazaroni (from Brazil) and Jupp Derwall and Sepp Piontek (from Germany)headed to the Golden Horn to help raise the standard of domestic competition in Turkey. And it was not long before they were joined by an increasing number of star players. Famous imports over the years have included

Romania's Gheorghe Hagi and Brazil's 1994 FIFA World Cup-winning goalkeeper Claudio Taffarel to current heroes such as Germany's Lukas Podolski and Dutchmen Wesley Sneijder and Robin van Persie.

The progress made in Turkish football can be seen in the recent performances of the national team. They appeared at the UEFA European Football Championship finals for the first time in 1996,

reached the quarter-finals in 2000 and then the semi-finals at both the FIFA World Cup in 2002 (in Japan and Korea) and, subsequently, at UEFA EURO 2008 (in Austria and Switzerland).

Their coach in 2008, Fatih Terim, regained the helm in 2013 following the team's failure to qualify for the 2014 FIFA World Cup finals. His task was a challenging one: to qualify from a group that also included the Netherlands, the Czech Republic and rapidly improving Iceland.

Turkey made a disappointing start, losing 3–0 to Iceland in Reykjavík, but home and away wins against Kazakhstan, plus a 1–1 draw away to the Dutch, thanks to a vital goal from Burak Yilmaz, kept them in the hunt.

The key result, however, was in September 2015, when the Turks entertained the Netherlands at Konya and raced into a 2–0 lead 30 minutes before winning 3–0. In a dramatic last round of matches, Turkey defeated already qualified Iceland 1–0 to snatch third place in the group and their ticket to France.

By this time Terim had established a settled team, from Volkan

Babacan in goal to experienced Gökhan Gönül at right-back and on to the Spain-based captain Arda Turan and newcomer Hakan Çalhanoğlu in midfield in support of Burak, who was the Turks' four-goal leading scorer in qualifying. The Galatasaray striker will be determined to increase his UEFA EURO 2016 tally in France.

TURKEY AT THE UEFA EURO FINALS

1960	Did not qualify
1964	Did not qualify
1968	Did not qualify
1972	Did not qualify
1976	Did not qualify
1980	Did not qualify
1984	Did not qualify
1988	Did not qualify
1992	Did not qualify
1996	Group stage
2000	Quarter-final
2004	Did not qualify
2008	Semi-final
2012	Did not qualify

EURO2016
FRANCE

GROUP D
CROATIA

A change of coach late in their qualifying campaign gave Croatia the boost in momentum the squad required, and now they head for the UEFA EURO 2016 finals with confidence renewed. France also has happy memories for Croatia: it was there that the country achieved its best-ever result in international football – third place at the 1998 FIFA World Cup.

COACH
ANTE ČAČIĆ

Aged 62, Ante Ćaćić is one of UEFA EURO 2016's coaching veterans. Born in Zagreb, Croatia, on 29 September 1953, he has been coaching for 30 years, since a first appointment with minor club Prigorje Markuševec in 1986. Ćaćić's first experience of Croatia's national team was as was part of the Under-21 staff in the late 1990s, and he also worked with Libya's youth teams from 2003 to 2006. Later appointments came with Croatia's record champions Dinamo Zagreb and Slovenia's Maribor. He became Croatia's national coach in autumn September 2015 to replace Niko Kovač after a 2–0 loss to Norway had threatened to derail Croatia's UEFA EURO 2016 qualifying campaign.

Croatia gained a high-profile role in European football within only a few years of the country obtaining its independence following the fragmentation of the former Yugoslavia in the early 1990s.

Until 1991, just 25 years ago, Croatia did not exist as an independent country. They became full members of UEFA and FIFA a year later. Although they did not make their tournament debut until UEFA EURO 96, their impact was immediate and huge, beating Italy and topping the qualifying group. Croatia went on to reach the quarter-finals of UEFA EURO 96, losing 2–1 to eventual champions Germany, and then stormed to third place at the 1998 FIFA World Cup in France. They played a classy brand of football in France – one that confirmed players such as Zvonimir Boban, Davor Šuker and Robert Prosinečki as being among the most gifted in the game.

Šuker, now head of the Croatia federation, proved that he was an

BELOW: Croatia left it late to qualify for UEFA EURO 2016, but a change of coach and wins in their final two Group H matches saw them leap-frog over Norway into second place behind Italy.

STAR PLAYER

IVAN RAKITIĆ

POSITION: **Midfielder** • CLUB: **Barcelona (Spain)** • AGE: **28**
BORN: **10 March 1988, Mohlin, Switzerland**
INTERNATIONAL DEBUT: **8 September 2007, v Estonia**
CAPS: **75** • GOALS: **10**

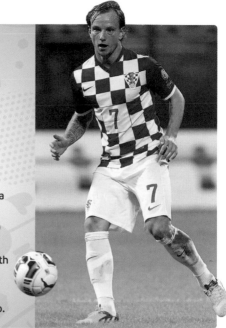

Ivan Rakitić's family moved to Switzerland before he was born and he raised there. His father and elder brother were both footballers, but Ivan was far better than both, breaking into FC Basel's senior team as a teenager. Although playing for Switzerland at youth levels, he chose to represent Croatia's senior national team. He starred at the UEFA EURO 2008 finals and was outstanding again at both UEFA EURO 2012 and the 2014 FIFA World Cup. His fine national team form was repeated with his clubs, Schalke 04 (in Germany) and Sevilla (in Spain), earning him a move to Barcelona in 2014. His first season with the Catalans ended with the treble of UEFA Champions League, the Spanish league and cup.

international superstar by scoring six goals to win the Golden Boot.

Only twice since then have Croatia's famous chequered red and white shirts not lit up the finals of a major international tournament. They missed out on UEFA EURO 2000 and failed to qualify for the 2010 FIFA World Cup finals.

Croatia were eliminated at the group stages in both 2004 and 2012, but in 2008, in Austria and Switzerland, they reached the quarter-finals. They were unlucky not to reach the last four after losing a dramatic clash to Turkey, on penalties after extra time, in Vienna.

Former international Nico Kovač led Croatia to the 2014 FIFA World Cup in Brazil, at which they had the honour of sharing the opening match with Brazil – and considered themselves unfortunate to lose to the hosts. However, Kovač was replaced by Ante Čačić in September 2015. Draws against Italy (twice) and Azerbaijan, followed by a defeat in Norway, left Croatia's hopes of automatic qualification for UEFA EURO 2016 looking a little slim.

A 3–0 home win over Bulgaria in Zagreb put Croatia back on track and a concluding 1–0 win over Malta

in Valletta saw them secure the runners-up spot in Group H behind Italy – thanks also, and significantly, to Norway's simultaneous defeat in Italy.

Italian-based midfielder or striker Ivan Perišić held the key to Croatia's qualification. He scored their first goal in the victory over Bulgaria and then the decisive single goal in Malta. Perišić, who is with Internazionale in Milan, ended as the group's six-goal leading marksman.

Unusually, though born in Split, he has not played at senior level in Croatia. He began his career in France, at Sochaux, moved to Club Brugge in Belgium, then to Borussia Dortmund and Wolfsburg in Germany before moving to Inter in 2015.

However, Croatia are far from being a one-man team. Ivan Rakitić and Luka Modrić, from Spanish rivals Barcelona and Real Madrid respectively, are two of the most talented midfielders in the European game. Rakitić was a key member of the Barcelona side that won the UEFA Champions League final against Juventus in Berlin in 2015.

Supporting experience has been provided by defenders Vedran Ćorluca, Danijel Pranjić and

Croatia's most-capped player Darijo Srna, along with forwards Mario Mandžukić and Ivica Olić. All have won well over 50 caps for Croatia, while Srna and Olić are two members of the country's five-man "centenary" club.

Croatia's big-match experience could well be of vital importance in their quest for success in France.

CROATIA AT THE UEFA EURO FINALS

1960	Did not exist
1964	Did not exist
1968	Did not exist
1972	Did not exist
1976	Did not exist
1980	Did not exist
1984	Did not exist
1988	Did not exist
1992	Did not exist
1996	Quarter-final
2000	Did not qualify
2004	Group stage
2008	Quarter-final
2012	Group stage

Spain's qualification for UEFA EURO 2016 was expected and their rebuilt squad, featuring new faces and veterans of two EURO victories and a FIFA World Cup success, won nine out of ten Group C matches, scoring 24 goals in the process.

GROUP E
BELGIUM

Belgium's Red Devils have made enormous progress over the past few years as their latest young generation of stars have gained in experience and confidence. Having suffered just a single defeat in qualifying, and having reached No.1 in the FIFA World Rankings for the first time, Marc Wilmots will be taking a squad to the UEFA EURO 2016 finals that is brimming with confidence.

COACH
MARC WILMOTS

Few men carry as much respect and status in modern Belgian football as Marc Wilmots. Born on 22 February 1969, he was a combative midfielder who scored 28 goals in 70 games for Belgium between 1990 and 2002 and played club football at home, in France with Bordeaux and in Germany with Schalke. After retiring, Wilmots entered politics as a senator before his return to football, and he has been laying down the law as manager of Belgium since May 2012, during which time he has been a father-figure coach to a highly talented new generation of Belgian footballers. He guided them to the quarter-finals of the 2014 FIFA World Cup in Brazil.

Belgium, with an association formed in 1895 and the second-oldest league outside Great Britain, was one of the driving forces behind the formation of FIFA and was one of only four European nations to travel to Uruguay to participate at the inaugural FIFA World Cup in 1930.

But, in comparison to their neighbours, the strictly amateur nature of the domestic game severely hindered the country's progress. The yoke of amateurism was only discarded in 1972, and the introduction of professionalism coincided with an immediate improvement in the fortunes of the national side.

From 1972 to 1984 Belgium made the last eight of four successive European Football Championships (only four teams made the finals in 1976), and in 1980 they reached the final for the first time, losing narrowly by 2–1 to West Germany in Rome.

The majority of that 1980 team went on to represent Belgium for the next decade and contained many

BELOW: One of the pre-tournament favourites, Belgium went into the draw for the UEFA EURO 2016 finals at the top of the FIFA World Rankings. They had taken over as World No. 1 last November.

STAR PLAYER
EDEN HAZARD

POSITION: **Winger** • CLUB: **Chelsea (England)** • AGE: **25**
BORN: **7 January 1991, La Louviere, Belgium**
INTERNATIONAL DEBUT: **18 November 2008, v Luxembourg**
CAPS: **62** • GOALS: **12**

Eden Hazard confirmed his long-evident potential in 2015 when his Premier League success with Chelsea was recognised when he won the league's top player awards from both the media and his fellow professionals. The son of two footballers, his youthful skill and speed brought him a cross-border career start at LOSC Lille, with whom he won the French double in 2011 before securing a £32 million move to Chelsea a year later. While the titles and awards piled up at club level, Hazard played a key role in the national team's revival, including a run to the quarter-finals of the 2014 FIFA World Cup, qualification for UEFA EURO 2016 and Belgium's rise to the top of the FIFA World Rankings.

of the country's most celebrated players, including goalkeeper Jean-Marie Pfaff, full-back Eric Gerets and 96-cap striker Jan Ceulemans. Their finest hour came at the 1986 FIFA World Cup finals, where they lost to Argentina in the semi-finals, with Enzo Scifo the star.

Belgium made history when they co-hosted UEFA EURO 2000 with the Netherlands, but were unable to rise to the occasion. They were knocked out in the first round, but learned from the experience and much the same team then progressed to the second round of the 2002 FIFA World Cup before falling to Brazil.

Qualifying for the UEFA Euro finals proved beyond them over the next decade. However, a rising new generation of highly talented youngsters emerged during those years and they demonstrated their prowess by reaching the quarter-finals of the 2014 FIFA World Cup before losing 1–0 to eventual tournament runners-up Argentina.

Even though he is only 22 years of age, Chelsea's Thibaud Courtois has established himself as one of Europe's most commanding goalkeepers. Premier League stalwarts Toby Alderweireld and Jan

Vertonghen from Tottenham and Vincent Kompany from Manchester City, plus Nicolas Lombaerts from Russia's Zenit have brought a defensive consistency Belgium lacked since the days of Eric Gerets and Walter Meeuws in the 1980s.

In midfield, coach Marc Wilmots has been spoiled for choice between Kevin Mirallas, Nacer Chadli, Marouane Fellaini and Axel Witsel, plus the highly creative Kevin de Bruyne and Eden Hazard on the wings. At the apex of attack a further threat on goal comes from the Liverpool pair Christian Benteke and Divock Origi.

De Bruyne and Hazard were Belgium's five-goal joint leading marksmen in qualifying, followed by Fellaini with four and Dries Mertens with three. Belgium won seven of their ten games, lost only one, scored 24 goals and conceded only five. They topped Group B with a two-point advantage over Wales and six ahead of Bosnia and Herzegovina who ended up in the playoffs.

The Red Devils got off to a comfortable 6–0 winning start against Andorra, but failed to build on it after being held 1–1 in Bosnia and 0–0

at home by Wales. Only in March of last year did they pick up speed again when two goals from Manchester United's Fellaini fired them to a 5–0 victory over Cyprus.

After that there was no looking back and Belgium ensured progress to the Euro finals for the first time in 16 years with a game to spare following a 4–1 win over Andorra.

BELGIUM AT THE UEFA EURO FINALS

1960	Did not enter
1964	Did not qualify
1968	Did not enter
1972	Third place
1976	Did not qualify
1980	Runners-up
1984	Group stage
1988	Did not qualify
1992	Did not qualify
1996	Did not qualify
2000	Group stage
2004	Did not qualify
2008	Did not qualify
2012	Did not qualify

GROUP E
ITALY

EURO 2016
FRANCE

Italy finished as UEFA EURO runners-up in both 2000 and 2012, and they are impatient to reclaim the crown they have not worn since they hosted the finals for the first time back in 1968. The test for coach Antonio Conte is to recreate the club success he achieved as both a player and then the boss of record champions Juventus with the national team.

COACH
ANTONIO CONTE

Antonio Conte took on the high-pressure role as national coach of the Azzurri in place of Cesare Prandelli following Italy's group-stage exit from the FIFA World Cup finals in Brazil in June 2014. Conte's qualifications were never in doubt. As a right-winger and then midfielder, he spent 13 successful years with Juventus, winning the UEFA Champions League, and appearing at the finals of both the UEFA European Football Championship and the FIFA World Cup. After retiring as a player, Conte, born in Lecce on 31 July 1969, raced back up the coaching ladder to lead Juve to three Serie A titles, one Coppa Italia and one Supercoppa. He has been voted Italy's Coach of the Year on three occasions.

Italy have won the FIFA World Cup four times, so they have plenty of ground to make up in the UEFA European Football Championship.

Apart from finishing fourth in 1980 and 1988 they were runners-up in 2000, quarter-finalists in 2008 and runners-up again last time around in 2012 against Spain. That was under the management of Claudio Prandelli the man who former Juventus coach Antonio Conte succeeded in 2014.

Conte's work as coach has been scrutinised relentlessly in a nation that is passionate about its football. But at least he can point to a comparatively smooth route through qualifying Group H. Italy finished top, four points ahead of Croatia and five points clear of third-placed Norway. Italy was one of three teams (along with England and Austria) to complete their ten-match schedule undefeated.

A typically parsimonious Italian defence conceded only seven goals, although Conte would have preferred his forwards to have scored more than the 16 goals they achieved. Graziano

BELOW: Beaten finalists at UEFA EURO 2012, Italy's target is to go one better in 2016 and their blend of youth and experience makes that goal very achievable.

STAR PLAYER
GIANLUIGI BUFFON

POSITION: **Goalkeeper** · CLUB: **Juventus (Italy)** · AGE: **38**
BORN: **28 January 1978, Carrara, Italy**
INTERNATIONAL DEBUT: **29 October 1997, v Russia**
CAPS: **152** · GOALS: **0**

"Gigi" Buffon has been Italy's No.1 since 1997 and a fixture among the world's top goalkeepers for nearly two decades. He made his name at Parma, with whom he won the UEFA Cup and Italian Supercup, before joining Juventus in 2001 for a fee of £32 million – a world record for a goalkeeper. He won two league titles and two supercups before hitting a career pinnacle when Italy won the 2006 FIFA World Cup. Buffon conceded only two goals in the finals, one an own goal, the other a penalty. A back injury ended his 2010 FIFA World Cup after 45 minutes, but he starred at national and club levels, and helped Juventus reach the 2015 UEFA Champions League final, where they lost 3–1 to Barcelona.

Pellè, the Southampton and former Feyenoord striker, was the Italians' three-goal leading scorer, vindicating Conte's confidence in him.

Although Pellè had starred for Italy at the FIFA Under-20 World Cup in 2005 and then in the 2007 Under-21 UEFA Football Championship, it was not until Conte took over as national coach that anyone showed faith in what Pellè might achieve at senior international level.

Elsewhere, Italy will bring the traditional mixture of experience and style to France, exemplified in captain and goalkeeper Gigi Buffon, who has been playing UEFA European Championship football for the past 17 years. In front of him in defence are Juventus rocks Giorgio Chiellini, Andrea Barzaglia and Leonardo Bonucci with clubmate Claudio Marchisio contributing his metronomic efforts in midfield.

The international retirement of Andrea Pirlo after Italy's FIFA World Cup adventure in Brazil ended in an early group-stage exit was a blow to the team's creativity. Therefore, much responsibility in qualifying rested on the shoulders of Lazio's Antonio Candreva and Marco Parolo and Milan's Riccardo Montolivo.

Notable former Italy sides (and standout managers) have set an extremely high standard for Conte's new Azzurri to match.

Under legendary coach Vittorio Pozzo, Italy lost only seven games in the 1930s, winning the FIFA World Cup in 1934 and 1938 as well as the 1936 Olympic title. The 1930s also saw the beginnings of a trend for Italian clubs to import foreign players, although a ban was imposed in the mid-1960s for fear that home-grown talent was being stifled.

The national side duly won the UEFA European title in 1968 and then reached the FIFA World Cup final two years later before losing to Brazil in a classic final in Mexico. Clubs such as Juventus and Milan dominated the 1970s and provided the foundation on which Enzo Bearzot built a FIFA World Cup-winning team in 1982.

Dino Zoff kept opponents at bay at one end of the pitch, while Paolo Rossi pounced for decisive goals at the other end. But Italy finished "only" third as hosts at the 1990 FIFA World Cup before pride was restored following Zoff's return in a new role as coach. Italy reached the UEFA EURO 2000 final and were within seconds

of glory when France snatched an equaliser that took the final to extra time and a golden-goal winner from striker David Trezeguet who was about to join Juventus.

They reached the final again eight years later, only to be defeated 4–0 by defending champions Spain in Kyiv. UEFA EURO 2016 could prove third time lucky for the Italians.

ITALY AT THE UEFA EURO FINALS

1960	Did not qualify
1964	Did not qualify
1968	WINNERS
1972	Did not qualify
1976	Did not qualify
1980	Fourth place
1984	Did not qualify
1988	Fourth place
1992	Did not qualify
1996	Group stage
2000	Runners-up
2004	Group stage
2008	Quarter-final
2012	Runners-up

REPUBLIC OF IRELAND

It is not only the Republic of Ireland's players who will be welcomed back to the UEFA European finals; so will their fans, whose positive enthusiasm always lights any tournament they attend. Under Martin O'Neill, the Irish are back for the third time on the major European stage and will be as confident as ever of causing an upset.

COACH
MARTIN O'NEILL

Born and brought up in Northern Ireland, Martin O'Neill made his teenage name locally with Distillery. His potential brought a move to England's Nottingham Forest with whom he won the UEFA Champions Cup under Brian Clough. O'Neill also played 64 games for Northern Ireland whom he captained at the 1982 FIFA World Cup finals. O'Neill started out in management in the English non-league system and moved up to Norwich City and Leicester City before leading Scotland's Celtic to six trophies in five years. He returned to England with Aston Villa and Sunderland before taking the Republic of Ireland job in 2013 in succession to Giovanni Trapattoni.

The Republic of Ireland took the play-off route to the UEFA EURO 2016 party, defeating Bosnia-Herzegovina 3–1 on aggregate having finished in third place in qualifying Group D behind world champions Germany and Poland.

Two vital goals from Stoke City midfielder Jon Walters proved to be the difference between the two teams and it underlined the reliance that Ireland has placed on players who earn their living playing in England and Scotland.

That was always considered a decisive bar to Ireland appearing at the major finals tournaments. But all that changed in 1986, when Jack Charlton, a FIFA World Cup winner with England in 1966, became coach.

He utilized the physical strength, determination and skills his players had perfected in the English league to give the side belief in itself. In 1988, they qualified for the UEFA European Football Championship finals. Unfortunately, Liam Brady, perhaps the greatest Republic player in history,

BELOW: The Republic of Ireland were grouped with FIFA World Cup winners Germany in the qualifiers and at UEFA EURO 2016, they will have to play the nation ranked No. 1 by FIFA in 2015, Belgium.

STAR PLAYER
ROBBIE KEANE

POSITION: **Striker** · CLUB: **Los Angeles Galaxy (United States)** · AGE: **35**
BORN: **8 July 1980, Dublin, Ireland**
INTERNATIONAL DEBUT: **25 March 1998, v Czech Republic**
CAPS: **143** · GOALS: 67

Robbie Keane was a member of the Irish Republic's own "golden generation" when they won the UEFA Under-16 and Under-18 European titles in 1998. A year later, having already made his senior international debut, he was playing at the FIFA Youth World Cup. Keane scored three goals in Ireland's four games at the 2002 FIFA World Cup and has progressed to become Ireland's all-time record marksman with 67 goals in 143 matches. He is also the world game's highest-scoring current international and the fifth-highest in European history. Keane's scoring talent also earned him an intimidating record in club football in Europe before he moved to LA Galaxy in 2011.

missed the tournament and thus never displayed his exquisite passes on the big stage. The Republic failed to progress beyond the group stage, but they did take a notable scalp when they beat England 1–0 in their opening game.

Having made the initial breakthrough, the Republic continued to make progress and qualified for the 1990 FIFA World Cup finals in Italy. No matter that the hosts beat them with a solitary goal in the quarter-finals, the Republic had arrived.

They narrowly missed out on a place at the UEFA EURO 1992 finals in Sweden, but succeeded – where England, Scotland, Wales and Northern Ireland all failed – in qualifying for the 1994 FIFA World Cup finals, at which they reached the second round. It was a performance they repeated at the 2002 FIFA World Cup finals under manager Mick McCarthy. They came to within a penalty shootout (against Spain) of reaching the quarter-finals.

Ireland qualified for the UEFA European Football Championship finals in Poland and Ukraine in 2012, but were unable to progress beyond

the group stage. They then failed to qualify for the 2014 FIFA World Cup in Brazil. This led to a change of management, with the departure of the veteran Italian, Giovanni Trapattoni, and the arrival of O'Neill who had been a FIFA World Cup player with Northern Ireland.

O'Neill has a solid pillar of experienced players, mostly from the English Premier League. Defender John O'Shea has won a century of international caps during an outstanding club career with Manchester United and now Sunderland, while Everton's Aiden McGeady and Stoke's Glenn Whelan have been regulars in midfield for most of the past decade.

Captain Robbie Keane, in attack, has long been extending his records as Ireland's record cap-winner and marksman, but is not the only threat to opposing defences. Southampton's Shane Long has a knack of scoring vital goals and Walters was the hero against Bosnia-Herzegovina.

Ireland began their qualifying campaign with McGeady scoring both goals in a 2–1 away win to Georgia in Tbilisi, while a late goal from O'Shea earned a fine 1–1 draw away

to Germany. However, a defeat by Scotland was followed by costly draws against Poland and the Scots.

Long scored the only goal against Germany in Dublin for a famous victory, but a last-game 2–1 loss to Poland – had they won they would have qualified automatically – meant a play-off place instead.

REPUBLIC OF IRELAND AT THE UEFA EURO FINALS

1960	Did not qualify
1964	Did not qualify
1968	Did not qualify
1972	Did not qualify
1976	Did not qualify
1980	Did not qualify
1984	Did not qualify
1988	Group stage
1992	Did not qualify
1996	Did not qualify
2000	Did not qualify
2004	Did not qualify
2008	Did not qualify
2012	Group stage

GROUP E
SWEDEN

Zlatan Ibrahimović's ability to mark the big occasions with dramatic goals will make Sweden one of the great attractions at UEFA EURO 2016. He should feel at home, not only because he plays his club football in France, but also because he knows all about the EURO finals from his goal-scoring experiences in both 2008 and 2012.

COACH

ERIK HAMRÉN

Fifty-eight-year-old Erik Hamrén built his reputation both in Sweden and abroad before he was finally appointed as Sweden's national coach in 2009 in succession to Lars Lagerbäck. Earlier, he had won the Swedish cup with both AIK Solna and Örgryte IS before moving to Denmark, where he won the league title with Aalborg BK and was also voted Manager of the Year. In 2008, he moved to Norway and won the championship there twice with Rosenborg BK when he initially took up the role of Sweden coach on a part-time basis until 2010. Sweden missed out on qualification for the 2014 FIFA World Cup, so France represents an opportunity to make up for lost time for Hamrén's Sweden.

Sweden have been Scandinavia's top national side since the 1920s, and have a deserved reputation for producing quality players. But none of those players has made a worldwide impression to compare with that of Ibrahimović who will lead their campaign in France.

Sweden made international their debut in 1908 and entered the first four Olympic tournaments – with mixed success. That era, however, produced the man who, pre-Zlatan, had been the country's greatest striker: Sven Rydell, who scored a then-record 49 goals in 43 games.

Sweden were at their best in the late 1940s when they boasted one of the most famous forward lines in history. Gunnar Gren, Gunnar Nordahl and Nils Liedholm – the "Gre-No-Li" trio – sparked Sweden to Olympic gold in 1948 and were promptly signed up by AC Milan, where they enjoyed further success.

Swedish players were regularly bought by European clubs, but were then barred from the national side by the strictly amateur rules of the association. Despite this handicap,

BELOW: No Swedish team can be under-estimated if their ranks include Zlatan Ibrahmović (back row, far right), one of the most brilliant strikers in world football.

STAR PLAYER
ZLATAN IBRAHIMOVIĆ

POSITION: **Centre-forward** · CLUB: **Paris Saint-Germain (France)** ·
AGE: **34** · BORN: **3 October 1981, Malmö, Sweden**
INTERNATIONAL DEBUT: **31 January 2001, v Faroe Islands**
CAPS: **111** · GOALS: **62**

Zlatan Ibrahimović has proved himself, time and again, as one of the most outstanding players in modern European football. His remarkable achievements for both clubs and country have been laced with some of the most spectacular of goals, season on season. "Ibra" began with home-town club Malmö FF, then won league titles, remarkably, in four other countries: Netherlands (with AFC Ajax), Italy (Juventus, FC Internazionale Milano and AC Milan), Spain (FC Barcelona) and, most recently, France (Paris Saint-Germain). He also won a host of top scorer and player of the year awards – including ten Footballer of the Year prizes in Sweden. He is also Sweden's all-time top scorer, with 62 goals in 111 appearances.

Sweden finished third at the 1950 FIFA World Cup, with Lennart "Nacka" Skoglund the new star.

The ban on professionals was lifted in time for the 1958 FIFA World Cup finals, which Sweden hosted, and with all their players available they reached the final. A decline followed in the 1960s, but Sweden qualified for all three FIFA World Cup finals tournaments in the 1970s, with defender Björn Nordqvist clocking up a then record 115 appearances between 1963 and 1978.

The clubs, too, began to make an impact, and Malmö FF reached the UEFA European Cup final in 1979. IFK Göteborg enjoyed the greatest success, though, winning the UEFA Cup twice (in 1982 and 1987) – as part-timers, because Sweden still has not yet introduced full professionalism.

Sweden's first appearance in the UEFA European Football Championship finals came in 1992, by virtue of being hosts, but they were beaten in the semi-finals by Germany. They followed up by finishing third in the 1994 FIFA World Cup, missed out on UEFA EURO 96, but have been ever-presents at the tournament finals since then.

The group stage was the beginning and end of the road in 2000. Sweden progressed to the quarter-finals in 2004, but were then unable to reach the knockout rounds in 2008 and 2012. Coincidentally, Sweden's Erik Hamrén, Spain's Vicente Del Bosque, England's Roy Hodgson and Germany's Joachim Low are the only four managers returning to the finals with the same countries.

Continuity, for Hamrén, has meant a squad with enormous know-how. Four have made more than 80 international appearances: goalkeeper Andreas Isaksson, midfielders Kim Källström and Sebastian Larsson and, of course, Ibrahimović. Not far behind them, in terms of international caps, are defenders Andreas Granqvist and Mikael Lustig, midfielder Pontus Wernbloom and forward Ola Toivonen. As for bright new talent pushing for recognition, striker John Guidetti and goalkeeper Patrik Carlgren were UEFA European Under-21 Championship winners in the Czech Republic in 2015.

After steady progress through qualifying Group G, Sweden slipped up badly with a 4–1 home defeat by Austria in September 2015. Victories over Liechtenstein and

Moldova were not enough to lift them into second place, so they were challenged to defeat southern neighbours Denmark in the play-offs

Appropriately, Ibrahimović, Sweden's eight-goal top scorer in the qualifying campaign, scored three times in the 4–3 aggregate triumph, two in the 2–2 second-leg draw, which rewarded, finally, all their hard work.

SWEDEN AT THE UEFA EURO FINALS

1960	Did not enter
1964	Did not qualify
1968	Did not qualify
1972	Did not qualify
1976	Did not qualify
1980	Did not qualify
1984	Did not qualify
1988	Did not qualify
1992	Semi-finals
1996	Did not qualify
2000	Group stage
2004	Quarter-finals
2008	Group stage
2012	Group stage

When Belgium qualified for UEFA EURO 2016 with a 4–1 victory in Andorra, playmaking midfielder Eden Hazard, 10, started, scored, missed a penalty, was substituted and finished off the night as a megaphone-toting cheerleader.

GROUP F
PORTUGAL

Cristiano Ronaldo ranks among the greatest players of all time after his remarkable goal-scoring exploits with Real Madrid, Manchester United and Portugal. Now aged 31, the man from Madeira is approaching yet another major challenge – to inspire Portugal to win a major international title for the first time in their history.

COACH

FERNANDO SANTOS

Born in Lisbon on 10 October 1954, Fernando Santos never played high-level football, retiring at 21 in 1975 after realising he would not make the grade. Instead, he graduated in electrical engineering before being lured back to the game with former club Estoril-Praia. His coaching career took off with spells at FC Porto, AEK, Panathinaikos FC and PAOK FC in Greece, as well as with Lisbon rivals Sporting and Benfica. He turned to national team football with Greece in 2010 and led them to the quarter-finals of UEFA EURO 2012 and then to the second round of the 2014 FIFA World Cup in Brazil. Following the latter tournament, he was appointed manager of Portugal, succeeding Paulo Bento.

Portugal bounced back from the disappointment of crashing out at the group stages of the 2014 FIFA World Cup to qualify in style, ultimately, for the UEFA EURO 2016 finals. Along the way, they also defeated Argentina and Italy in friendlies along the way – opponents they had not managed to defeat at senior level for more than 40 years.

Above all, Portugal head to France hoping to benefit from the full fitness of their captain and leading marksman Cristiano Ronaldo, whose injury handicap had played such a crucial role in their group-stage elimination in Brazil.

Ronaldo spearheads a squad that is being increasingly strengthened by a new young swathe of players, whose talents have drawn comparisons to the so-called "golden generation" that featured the likes of Luis Figo, Rui Costa and Paulo Sousa who won the FIFA World Youth Cup in 1989 and 1991.

In 2015, Portugal finished runners-up to Sweden (on penalties)

BELOW: The presence of Cristiano Ronaldo (back row, far right) in any team makes them a dangerous opponent and every team in Group F will be fully aware of his incredible football talent.

STAR PLAYER
CRISTIANO RONALDO

POSITION: **Forward** • CLUB: **Real Madrid (Spain)** • AGE: **31**
BORN: **5 February 1985, Funchal, Madeira**
INTERNATIONAL DEBUT: **20 August 2003, v Kazakhstan**
CAPS: **123** • GOALS: **55**

Cristiano Ronaldo vies with Lionel Messi for the status of the world's best player. Winner of FIFA's Ballon d'Or in 2008, 2013 and 2014, he cost Real Madrid €85 million from Manchester United in 2009 and has repaid the investment with a record tally of goals. His club honours include four league titles in England and Spain, many domestic cups, and the UEFA Champions League and FIFA Club World Cup with United and Real. Ronaldo also holds the record for most goals (17) in a single UEFA Champions League campaign (in 2013–14). His 13-year career with Portugal has seen him star at three UEFA European Football Championships and three FIFA World Cups and Ronaldo was three-goal co-top scorer at UEFA EURO 2012.

at the UEFA European Under-21 Championship finals, and several of the players who starred in that tournament are likely to feature in France, most notably AS Monaco FC's nimbly skilful playmaker Bernardo Silva and anchor man William Carvalho from Sporting Clube of Lisbon.

At the other end of the experience scale, goalkeepers Rui Patricio and Eduardo share around 80 caps between them behind a defence that has formed in the heat of big-occasion challenges, with players such as Bruno Alves, Ricardo Carvalho and the Real Madrid CF pair Pepe and Fábio Coentrão.

Coach Fernando Santos has varied his tactics between 4-4-2 and 4-3-3, with João Moutinho, Miguel Veloso and Tiago Mendes providing midfield options while balancing defensive work with attacking expertise. The attacking weapons ahead of them comprise Nani and Ronaldo, old friends and former club-mates at Manchester United.

Ronaldo was Portugal's five-goal leading marksman in qualifying Group I. His first goal was crucial, because it brought a 1–0 win in Denmark after Portugal had opened

their campaign with a surprise defeat at home to Albania in Aveiro. The victory in Copenhagen was the first of seven in a row, including a 1–0 win over the Danes in the return home fixture. A second-half goal from João Moutinho secured their place at the top of the table.

No one doubts that Portugal will present stern opposition in the finals, not least after having reached the semi-finals four years ago in Poland and Ukraine, when they lost to champions and eventual winners Spain on penalties.

But Portugal, who have come so close so often, still await that elusive first senior trophy. The great Eusébio, Mário Coluna, José Augusto and their team-mates finished third at the 1966 FIFA World Cup and then fourth in 2006.

When they have qualified, Portugal have always progressed beyond the group stage at the UEFA European Football Championships. They reached the semi-finals in 1984, 2000 and 2012 and the quarter-finals in 1996 and 2008.

Most memorably, though, as tournament hosts in 2004, they reached the final under manager

Luiz Felipe Scolari. Portugal, lining up with the veteran Luis Figo and the explosive newcomer Ronaldo, were clear favourites to win against Greece in the Estédio da Luz in Lisbon. However, a goal from Angelos Charisteas early in the second half left them bitterly disappointed.

That painful memory should serve as extra motivation in France.

PORTUGAL AT THE UEFA EURO FINALS

1960	Did not qualify
1964	Did not qualify
1968	Did not qualify
1972	Did not qualify
1976	Did not qualify
1980	Did not qualify
1984	Semi-final
1988	Did not qualify
1992	Did not qualify
1996	Quarter-final
2000	Semi-final
2004	Runners-up
2008	Quarter-final
2012	Semi-final

GROUP F
ICELAND

UEFA EURO 2016 represents an exciting adventure for Iceland men's team, who have never previously reached the finals of a major international tournament. Their qualification illustrates the progress they have achieved over the past 50 years – it wasn't too long ago when it was rare to see even individual Icelandic players in the continental game.

COACH
LARS LAGERBÄCK

Lars Lagerbäck is enjoying a second successful career as a national team coach. Lagerbäck, born on 16 July 1948, managed the Swedish national team from 1998 to 2009 when they were regular qualifiers for the finals of both the FIFA World Cup and the UEFA European Championship. He stepped down after Sweden missed out on qualification for the 2010 FIFA World Cup, but subsequently went to the finals as manager of Nigeria. He returned to the national team arena with Iceland in October 2011 when he succeeded Olafur Johannesson. His contract expires after Iceland's historic appearance in France, after which he will be succeeded by his Icelandic assistant, Heimir Hallgrímsson.

Although one of Europe's smaller nations, in terms of registered players and coaches, Iceland have regularly proved capable of upsetting European football's bigger fish.

The game in Iceland can be traced back to 1894, when it was introduced by a Scottish printer and bookseller James Ferguson. An "Athletic Union" and national championship were established in 1912. KR Reykjavik were the first champions, and have a record 26 titles to their credit. Teams met only once a season in the league until the more usual home and away format was introduced in 1959. KR, as with the first-ever title, won in 1959, and

followed up by winning the inaugural Icelandic cup a year later. In 1964, KR also became the first Icelandic club to test the competitive waters in Europe.

By then, Iceland's national team had been testing its mettle for 18 years. They made their international debut on 17 July 1946 with a 3–0 home defeat to Denmark – the country from which Iceland had secured its independence only two years earlier. The first victory came in 1947, a 2–0 win over Finland in Reykjavík, and their debut in FIFA World Cup qualifying came in 1957 (for the 1958 tournament). The team of the 1950s included their first star player, Albert Gudmundsson, who later

BELOW: Seventy years after their international debut and 60 years after appearing in their first qualifying competition, this Iceland squad will be the first to compete in an international tournament finals.

STAR PLAYER
GYLFI SIGURDSSON

POSITION: **Midfielder** • CLUB: **Swansea (Wales)** • AGE: **26**
BORN: **9 September 1989, Reykjavík, Iceland**
INTERNATIONAL DEBUT: **29 May 2010 v Andorra**
CAPS: **32** • GOALS: **11**

Gylfi Sigurdsson is one of the most consistently effective creative midfielders in England's Premier League and is a noted specialist from set pieces. He did not play senior football in Iceland, having moved to England as teenager with Reading in 2005. Sigurdsson turned professional there, but moved to Germany with Hoffenheim in 2010, returning to the Premier League with Swansea two years later. Apart from a brief spell at Tottenham, he has been based at the Liberty Stadium ever since. On the international stage, Sigurdsson represented Iceland at Under-17, Under-19 and Under-21 levels before making his senior debut in 2010, rapidly becoming a permanent fixture in the team.

played for Arsenal, AC Milan and AS Nancy-Lorraine in France. A statue of him now stands in front of the Icelandic Federation's offices.

A number of Icelandic players have made their mark abroad since then, including defender and later national coach Atli Edvaldsson at Fortuna Düsseldorf, striker Pétur Pétursson at Feyenoord and midfield general Ásgeir Sigurvinsson in Belgium and then Germany with Standard Liège and Stuttgart.

Football history was made in the spring of 1996, when a father and son, Arnór and Eidur Smári Gudjohnsen, both played for the national team in a friendly against Estonia.

Eidur Gudjohnsen, who went on to become his country's 25-goal record top scorer, would underline Icelandic football's potential by enjoying striking success with both Chelsea and Barcelona. Midfielder Gylfi Sigurdsson, at Swansea, is one of the most respected creative players currently starring in the English Premier League.

One of the most successful of early imported national coaches was Englishman Tony Knapp in the mid-1970s and was succeeded by former West German FIFA World Cup

striker Sigi Held. Progress within the domestic game meant that Iceland had home-grown coaches for two decades, until Sweden's Lars Lagerbäck was hired in 2011 to bring his international experience to bear.

Iceland reached the qualifying play-offs for the 2014 FIFA World Cup, but Croatia dashed their finals dream with a 2–0 aggregate victory. However, coming so close to qualifying instilled extra confidence in the squad for the UEFA EURO 2016 campaign. And they made no mistake his time.

They opened their Group A campaign with a 3–0 home win over Turkey, won away to Latvia and then 2–0 at home to the Netherlands third-place finishers at the FIFA World Cup three months earlier. Iceland's only two defeats came away to group winners the Czech Republic and to Turkey in the final qualifying game, by which time Iceland were already assured a place in France.

Sigurdsson not only commanded Iceland's attack, but also ended as the group's six-goal leading marksman. Other key players along the way included defenders Birkir Már Sævarsson and Ragnar Sigurdsson, captain Aron Gunnarsson in

midfield and Kolbeinn Sigthórsson and Alfred Finnbogason in attack.

Lagerbäck's coaching philosophy is to encourage players to gain confidence through taking responsibility. He believes once players cross the white line and run on to the pitch, the outcome of a game is down to them. Iceland's presence in France is his vindication.

ICELAND AT THE UEFA EURO FINALS

1960	Did not enter
1964	Did not qualify
1968	Did not enter
1972	Did not enter
1976	Did not qualify
1980	Did not qualify
1984	Did not qualify
1988	Did not qualify
1992	Did not qualify
1996	Did not qualify
2000	Did not qualify
2004	Did not qualify
2008	Did not qualify
2012	Did not qualify

AUSTRIA

Austria are one of European football's great traditional nations but it is a long time since they were regular contenders on the grand stage. This time, however, they will be dangerous outsiders after a remarkable qualifying campaign achieved by a team astutely managed by Marcel Koller and inspired by full-back or midfielder David Alaba.

COACH

MARCEL KOLLER

Swiss coach Marcel Koller had never played or coached in Austria before he was appointed national coach in November 2011 to succeed Didi Constantini after they had failed to qualify for UEFA EURO 2012. Koller, born in Zurich on 11 November 1960, had spent his entire playing career "at home" with Grasshopper Club, with whom he won seven Swiss league titles and five cups. His 56-cap national team career included appearances at UEFA EURO 96. As a coach, Koller worked at FC Wil 1990 before winning Swiss titles with both FC St Gallen and Grasshopper. Spells in Germany with 1FC Koln and VfL Bochum preceded his appointment as only Austria's third foreign coach in 30 years.

Marcel Koller has managed to achieve remarkable transformation of Austria's national team since being appointed coach in 2011. His selection came as a surprise to many fans and club officials who had agitated for a bigger "name" after the team's failure to qualify for the UEFA EURO 2012 finals.

Koller's challenge was to create a unity of spirit and purpose in a squad of players drawn from clubs all around the continent, with the only home-based regular player being Rapid Vienna goalkeeper Robert Almer.

Austria fell short in the 2014 FIFA World Cup qualifying competition, finishing third in their group behind Germany and Sweden, and the Swedes lay in wait for them again in the UEFA EURO 2016 preliminaries. They drew 1–1 in Vienna in the opening game of Group G – and those turned out to be the only points Koller's team dropped throughout the entire qualifying campaign.

They won every one of their nine subsequent games, including 1–0 victories both home and away against Russia, who finished eight

BELOW: Austria's qualification for the UEFA EURO 2016 finals was certainly helped by having a very settled squad, but nine wins and a draw in ten Group G games was an exceptional achievement.

STAR PLAYER
DAVID ALABA

POSITION: **Full-back / Midfield** • CLUB: **FC Bayern Munich (Germany)**
AGE: **23** • BORN: **24 June 1992, Vienna, Austria**
INTERNATIONAL DEBUT: **14 October 2009, v France**
CAPS: **41** • GOALS: **10**

David Alaba has had an explosive impact on the Austrian national team since he became his country's youngest-ever international when he made his debut against France in 2002 at the tender age of 17. His versatility has seen him appear on the wing, in midfield and at left-back. He rose to prominence as a youth player with FK Austria before moving to FC Bayern in 2008. In February 2010, he became Bayern's youngest-ever competitive player and, a month later, still only 17, he was playing in the UEFA Champions League. His penalty was the first of Austria's four goals in the win over Sweden in September 2015 that secured their place at UEFA EURO 2016.

points adrift as group runners-up. Rubin Okotie scored the winner in the first game in Vienna, with Marc Janko firing in the winner in the return fixture in Moscow.

Only England, with ten victories out of ten, had a better qualifying record than Koller's men, for whom lone striker Marc Janko was their seven-goal leading marksman.

One of the keys to Austria's success was their ability to pick a settled side. Almer, defenders Florian Klein, Aleksandar Dragovic and captain Christian Fuchs in defence, plus Zlatko Junuzovic and Marko Arnautovic in midfield, all played in every one of the ten qualifying matches.

Koller used only 17 players in total. One of the most important was Bayern Munich's David Alaba. Bundesliga fans were mostly used to seeing Alaba playing at left-back, but Koller has relied on him as the controller of Austria's game out of the midfield engine room. Remarkably, UEFA EURO 2016 will be Alaba's first senior tournament.

In fact, this is the first time Austria have actually qualified for the UEFA EURO finals. Their only

previous appearance, in 2008, was as co-hosts along with Switzerland and then they were eliminated in the first round group stage. Fans have to go even further back, to 1998, to remember Austria appearing at the FIFA World Cup finals.

Yet Austria – and Vienna, more particularly – was the focal point of continental European football in the first half of the last century. In 1902, Austria beat Hungary 5–0 at the Prater Stadium in what remains international football's second-oldest regular fixture after England v Scotland.

The inter-war period was Austria's most successful era, when the Wunderteam – led by Matthias Sindelar – swept all before them. In 30 matches from 1931 to 1934, Austria scored 101 goals, and the 1934 FIFA World Cup seemed to be at their mercy. But a defeat in the semi-final by hosts Italy ended their dreams.

A new side came together in the 1950s, led by Ernst Ocwirk and Gerhard Hanappi, but after reaching the FIFA World Cup finals in 1954 a decline set in – one that reached a nadir in 1991 when

the Faroe Islands, playing their first-ever competitive match, won 1–0 in a UEFA European Football Championship qualifier.

The road back to international respectability has been a long and difficult one, but, particularly considering their qualifying record, no one dare doubt Austria's right to be back up among the elite at last.

AUSTRIA AT THE UEFA EURO FINALS

1960	Did not qualify
1964	Did not qualify
1968	Did not qualify
1972	Did not qualify
1976	Did not qualify
1980	Did not qualify
1984	Did not qualify
1988	Did not qualify
1992	Did not qualify
1996	Did not qualify
2000	Did not qualify
2004	Did not qualify
2008	Group stage
2012	Did not qualify

GROUP F
HUNGARY

Hungary's revived national team picked themselves up impressively to reach the UEFA EURO 2016 finals via the play-offs. Manager Bernd Storck mixes his German knowhow with Hungary's proud football heritage and he has put together a squad that possesses renewed self-belief based on wise old heads in defence and bright new starlets in attack.

COACH

BERND STORCK

German Bernd Storck is one of the small band of "foreign" coaches at UEFA EURO 2016. He played in the Bundesliga with VfL Bochum and Borussia Dortmund, winning the cup in his last season (1989). After several roles as a coaching assistant, Storck – born in Herne on 25 January 1964 – built his career outside of Germany, notably in Kazakhstan with FC Almaty (in 2008) and the country's national youth teams. He spent two years in Greece with Olympiacos FC before moving to Hungary, initially as the country's Under-20 coach. He guided them to the knockout stages of the 2015 FIFA Under-20 World Cup which earned him a promotion to coach of the senior team on his return. His staff includes UEFA EURO 1996 winner (with Germany), Andreas Möller.

Hungary are one of the most welcome of finalists, their appearance in France demonstrating that, after years in the international shadows, the Magyar game is regaining its old verve and pride.

The cherry red shirts have featured at the finals on only two previous occasions, finishing third and fourth. Unfortunately, those appearances came way back in the early days of the original UEFA Nations Cup, in 1964 and 1972 respectively.

Hungary have not been in the UEFA European Football Championship finals for 44 years and have not featured at the FIFA World Cup since 1986. The days since they were consistent medal contenders at the Olympic Games have also long gone. Finally, however, following a 3–1 aggregate victory over Norway in the UEFA EURO 2016 play-offs, they are back in from the cold.

German manager Bernd Storck only took over in the summer of 2015, stepping up from his leadership of the Under-20 side to succeed Pál Dárdai. Initial results in qualifying in Group F were not

BELOW: The play-off defeat of Norway ended Hungary's 30-year wait to appear in another major tournament finals. When they last qualified in UEFA EURO competition, the finals comprised four teams.

STAR PLAYER
ZOLTAN GERA

POSITION: **Midfield** • CLUB: **Ferencváros (Hungary)** • AGE: **37**
BORN: **22 April 1979, Pecs, Hungary**
INTERNATIONAL DEBUT: **13 February 2002, v Switzerland**
CAPS: **86** • GOALS: **24**

Zoltán Gera, a winger or attacking midfielder, would have totalled more than a century of international appearances had it not been for injuries and a brief retirement from the national team between 2009 and 2010. He has delighted fans at home with Pecs and Ferencváros as well as in England with Fulham and West Bromwich Albion (spending two spells at the latter club). He has been voted Hungarian Footballer on the Year on three occasions and won a fans' award after leading Fulham to the final of the UEFA Europa League in 2010. He returned to Hungary with Ferencváros in 2014. In 2015, Gera and Ferencváros won the cup to add to the two league titles and two cups he won during his first spell with the club.

promising: Hungary were held by both Romania and Northern Ireland, beat the Faroe Islands and then lost to Greece. Only then did they pull themselves together to see off the Norwegians and return to the European finals at long last.

Storck has stepped into intimidating shoes. Highly respected predecessors such as Károly Dietz, Gusztáv Sebes, Márton Bukovi, Lajos Baróti, Rudolf Illovszky and György Mezey had taken Hungary to the very top of the international game.

Most famous of all was the "Magical Magyars" side of the early 1950s under Sebes: they had lost only one international in five years and were firm favourites to win the 1954 FIFA World Cup, before they fell short in the final. Stars such as Ferenc Puskás, Sándor Kocsis and József Bozsik still rank among the greatest footballers of all time. In 1953, they became the first non-British side to beat England at home, winning 6–3 at Wembley.

New stars emerged in the 1960s, such as Flórián Albert and Ferenc Bene, who led Hungary to the 1962 and 1966 FIFA World Cup quarter-finals and to Olympic gold in 1964 and 1968. Later came Tibor Nyilasi,

but then Hungarian football slipped into the international void from which it is only now re-emerging.

Only five of squad who saw off Norway in the play-offs were even born when Hungary last played on a major stage – at the 1986 FIFA World Cup in Mexico. They include veteran goalkeeper Gábor Király, now Hungary's most-capped player, who made his debut in 1998.

Not far behind him, in terms of service, are defenders, home-based Roland Juhász – with FC Videoton – and Vilmos Vanczák, who has been with Sion in Switzerland since 2007.

Ahead of them, responsible for turning defence into attack and mainly down the wings, have been Zoltan Gera and Balász Dzsudzsák.

Gera enjoyed many years in English football with Fulham and West Bromwich Albion, while Dzsudzsák has also spent the bulk of his club career abroad – in his case with PSV Eindhoven in the Netherlands, with FC Anji Makhachkala and FC Dinamo Moscow in Russia and most recently with Bursaspor in Turkey. Dzsudzsák ranks as the most expensive player in Hungary's history, having cost

Dinamo €19 million when he moved from Anji in 2012.

In attack Hungary look to widely-travelled Tamás Priskin as well as to newcomers such as László Kleinheisler. The Videoton youngster marked his debut by scoring the only goal in the play-off first leg against Norway. Hungary will hope there will be more to come from him in France.

HUNGARY AT THE UEFA EURO FINALS

1960	Did not qualify
1964	Third place
1968	Did not qualify
1972	Fourth place
1976	Did not qualify
1980	Did not qualify
1984	Did not qualify
1988	Did not qualify
1992	Did not qualify
1996	Did not qualify
2000	Did not qualify
2004	Did not qualify
2008	Did not qualify
2012	Did not qualify

Hungary were, for a decade (long before the advent of the FIFA world rankings), indisputably the world's best team, but they have made big strides since slipping to No.77 in the FIFA world rankings in 1997 and they ended 2015 at No.20, their best position for a quarter of a century.

Chapter 4
The History of the UEFA European Football Championship

HENRI DELAUNAY, FRENCH GENERAL SECRETARY OF NEWLY CREATED UEFA, WAS THE DRIVING FORCE BEHIND THE CREATION OF THE EUROPEAN CHAMPIONSHIP. ORIGINALLY IT WAS A KNOCKOUT COMPETITION AND JUST 17 NATIONS ENTERED THE FIRST EDITION OF THE TOURNAMENT THAT RAN BETWEEN 1958 AND 1960. THE LIKES OF ITALY, WEST GERMANY AND ENGLAND OPTED NOT TO ENTER THE INAUGURAL COMPETITION. THE TOURNAMENT'S FIRST-EVER MATCH CAME ON 28 SEPTEMBER 1958, AND SAW THE SOVIET UNION DEFEAT HUNGARY 3–1 IN MOSCOW. SPARTAK MOSCOW OUTSIDE-LEFT ANATOLY ILYIN CLAIMED THE HONOUR OF SCORING THE FIRST GOAL. FROM THAT POINT IT WAS ONWARDS AND UPWARDS.

Spain had to wait an agonising 44 years to win a second UEFA European Football Championship and then, in 2012, became the first nation to successfully defend the trophy. In between, they added the FIFA World Cup to cement their place as the undisputed best international team in world football at the time.

UEFA EUROPEAN NATIONS' CUP 1958–60

The Soviet Union carried off the inaugural UEFA European Nations' Cup. This was no surprise. They had been Olympic football champions in 1956 and had reached the quarter-finals on their FIFA World Cup debut in 1958.

France, still glowing from their third-place finish at the 1958 FIFA World Cup finals, had been initial favourites. They were also chosen to host the finals after reaching the last four, along with a Central and East European trio comprising the Soviet Union, Yugoslavia and Czechoslovakia.

The Soviet Union had enjoyed a bye into the finals. In the quarter-finals they had been drawn against Spain. But the Spanish government stepped in and refused to grant the team permission to travel to the Soviet Union, leaving the Soviet side with a walkover.

The finals in France comprised two knockout semi-finals, one third-place play-off match and the final itself.

France should have reached that final. In Paris they led Yugoslavia 4–2 in their semi-final opener with 15 minutes to play but relaxed, fatally. The Yugoslavs put three goals past French keeper Georges Lamia within three minutes. French fans could only excuse the result on the injury absences of playmaker Raymond Kopa and star striker Just Fontaine.

The Soviet Union, including legendary goalkeeper Lev Yashin, easily defeated Czechoslovakia 3–0 in Marseille in the other semi-final, with Valentin Ivanov scoring twice.

The final was played at the old Parc des Princes – just like the first European Champion Clubs' Cup final four years earlier. As had been the case with the club showdown, the referee was England's Arthur Ellis.

The first goal was almost an own goal, Soviet skipper Igor Netto deflecting a strike from Milan Galic, though the latter was credited with the goal just two minutes before the interval. Soviet right-wing Slava Metrevelli equalised after 49 minutes to send the final into extra time.

Yugoslavia had been the better team. Only the brilliance of Lev Yashin in the Soviet goal had denied them victory. But they lost heart and defensive discipline in extra time. Soviet centre-forward Viktor Ponedelnik snatched his one chance of the game ... and the Soviet Union became the first European champions.

ABOVE: Soviet Union captain Igor Netto, holding the trophy, followed by legendary goalkeeper Lev Yashin and the rest of the squad, acknowledge the Parisian crowd after winning the inaugural final.

UEFA EUROPEAN NATIONS' CUP 1962–64

Holders the Soviet Union were favourites to retain the UEFA European Nations' Cup in 1964. This time the finals were played in Spain and they proved something of a political triumph for football. In the 1960 quarter-finals, Spain withdrew from their tie against the Soviet Union. Four years on, Spain not only provided a host's welcome for the Soviet Union team but also met them in the final – and beat them.

Qualifying was still organised on a knockout basis, but this time with 29 countries competing. West Germany did not take part, but England entered for the first time ... and were instantly eliminated. Alf Ramsey's first competitive experience at international level ended in a 6–3 aggregate defeat (2–5 away and 1–1 at home) to a French team inspired by veteran Raymond Kopa.

Spain, under former Real and Atletico Madrid coach Jose Villalonga, were rebuilding. Villalonga had turned away from the dual-nationality stars, such as Alfredo di Stefano and Ferenc Puskás, and put his faith in youngsters emerging from Spain's unfashionable provincial clubs. They sounded a warning of what was to come in the first round with

ABOVE: Until EURO 2008, Spain's victory in the 1964 final was the country's only national team competition success and coach José Villalonga and captain Ferran Olivella were chaired off the pitch.

a 6–0 win over Romania. Valencia's Vicente Guillot scoring a hat-trick.

UEFA had designated Spain as hosts of the second edition's final phase, in which the Soviet Union lined up alongside Denmark and Hungary.

The Soviet Union launched the semi-finals by defeating Denmark, easily, by 3–0 in Barcelona. The other semi-final saw Spain defeat Hungary 2–1 after extra time. Real Madrid right-winger Amancio Amaro scored the winner five minutes from the end. Hungary's consolation was to beat Denmark for third place.

Amancio provided the eye-catching panache in Spain's attack, but their key player was midfield

general Luis Suárez. He came home for the finals after enjoying a superb season in Italy, during which he had inspired Internazionale to win the European Champions' Cup for the first time, against Amancio's Real Madrid.

Spain took an early lead in the final against the Soviet holders in the Estadio Bernabeu through Jesús Pereda. Galimzyan Khusainov hit back for the Soviet Union but a second-half strike from Zaragoza centre-forward Marcelino was the signal for the last Spanish national team celebrations until UEFA EURO 2008.

UEFA EUROPEAN FOOTBALL CHAMPIONSHIP 1966-68

In 1968, for the second successive tournament, the hosts – Italy, this time – ended up as champions. But the *Azzurri* needed a replay before defeating Yugoslavia who finished runners-up for the second time.

The dramatic success of the 1964 event was reflected in an increased entry for the 1968 edition of the tournament and UEFA's decision to organise the first round not on a knockout basis but in mini-leagues. The competition's name was also changed to the UEFA European Football Championship in time for the 1966–68 edition, reflecting its growing prestige.

One group comprised the British Home Championship. FIFA World Cup holders England finished one point clear of Scotland. Consolation for the latter came when they became the first nation to beat the newly crowned world champions, by 3–2 at Wembley, with goals from Denis Law, Bobby Lennox and Jim McCalliog.

The quarter-finals saw a reversion to the two-leg knockout system. The top tie was the meeting of world champions England and European champions Spain. An 84th-minute goal from Bobby Charlton handed England a narrow victory at Wembley. Spain levelled on aggregate in Madrid through Amancio Amaro, only for England to snap back seven minutes later through Martin Peters.

England were joined in the finals by hosts Italy, Yugoslavia and the Soviet Union. Italy had rebuilt after their defeat by North Korea at the 1966 FIFA World Cup. Yet it took a fortunate toss of a coin to secure their place in the final after their semi-final against the Soviet Union had finished goalless

ABOVE: Angelo Domenghini celebrates his last-minute equaliser for Italy in the EURO 68 final against Yugoslavia. It is the only final to go to a replay and Italy won the trophy at the second attempt, 2–0.

– the penalty shoot-out had yet to be introduced into top-level competition.

The other semi-final saw Yugoslavia win 1–0 against England, for whom midfielder Alan Mullery was sent off.

Yugoslavia took the lead against Italy in the final in Rome through left-winger Dragan Džajić, who also had scored against England. Angelo Domenghini equalised from a late free kick. Extra time was goalless, so the final went to a replay for the first and only time.

Exhausted Yugoslavia fell behind after 12 minutes when Gigi Riva struck. Pietro Anatasi added another on the half-hour. Italy held on and were European champions for the first time.

FOR THE RECORD

SEMI-FINALS
YUGOSLAVIA	1–0	England
ITALY	0–0	Soviet Union

(Italy won on toss of a coin after extra time)

THIRD-PLACE PLAY-OFF
ENGLAND	2–0	Soviet Union

FINAL (OLIMPICO, ROME)
Italy	1–1	Yugoslavia (AET)
Domenghini 80		*Dzajic 38*

REPLAY (OLIMPICO, ROME)
Italy	2–0	Yugoslavia
Riva 12		
Anastasi 31		

HT: 2–0
Att: 50,000
Ref: Ortiz de Mendibil (Spain)

Italy: Zoff, Salvadore, Burgnich, Guarneri, Facchetti, Rosato, Anastasi, Picchio, Domenghini, Mazzola, Riva.

Yugoslavia: Pantelić, Fazlagić, Paunović, Holcer, Damjanović, Aćimović, Trivić, Pavlović, Hošic, Musemić, Džajić.

UEFA EUROPEAN FOOTBALL CHAMPIONSHIP 1970–72

West Germany were the most outstanding side in the competition and duly collected their deserved reward for some superb football, a triumph that set them up to add the FIFA World Cup to their trophy cabinet two years later.

The nucleus of manager Helmut Schön's team came from Bayern Munich and Borussia Mönchengladbach. The creative combination of Bayern's revolutionary attacking sweeper, Franz Beckenbauer, and Borussia playmaker Günter Netzer, lit up the European game. The assistance of adventurous young left-back Paul Breitner and supreme marksman Gerd Müller ensured that the right team earned the crown.

Italy's attempt to retain the trophy was brought to an abrupt end in the quarter-finals by Belgium, who then won the vote to host the finals of the competition.

The first round was again played on a mini-league basis, this time featuring eight groups of four national teams. Then it was back to the two-leg, direct elimination quarter-finals.

The quarter-finals saw the Germans make history with their first victory at Wembley, where they overran their English hosts 3–1 before reaching the finals on the back of a goalless draw in West Berlin.

The remaining quarter-finals saw the Soviet Union maintain their dominance over Yugoslavia, Belgium prise loose Italy's grip on the Henri Delaunay trophy and Hungary squeeze past Romania after a play-off in Belgrade.

In the finals tournament, the semi-finals were split evenly between eastern and western Europe. Anderlecht's Parc Astrid was the venue for the Soviet Union's 1–0 defeat of Hungary, while Antwerp witnessed West Germany defeat hosts Belgium 2–1.

Belgium's consolation was to finish third after they beat Hungary three days later by 2–1 in the third-place play-off in Liege. Raoul Lambert from Brugge and Anderlecht's great Paul Van Himst scored the winners' goals.

In the final even a fine new Soviet team, built around a nucleus from the Ukraine club, Kyiv Dynamo, proved no match for the Germans. Netzer dominated midfield and hit a post before two typically opportunist strikes from Gerd Müller and another from Herbert Wimmer decided the final. Müller finished as the tournament's 11-goal top scorer.

FOR THE RECORD

SEMI-FINALS
SOVIET UNION	1–0	Hungary
WEST GERMANY	2–1	Belgium

THIRD-PLACE PLAY-OFF
BELGIUM	2–1	Hungary

FINAL (HEYSEL, BRUSSELS)
WEST GERMANY	3–0	Soviet Union

G. Müller 27, 57
Wimmer 52

HT: 1–0
ATT: 50,000
Ref: Marschall (Austria)

West Germany: Maier, Höttges, Beckenbauer, Schwarzenbeck, Breitner, Hoeness, Netzer, Wimmer, Heynckes, G. Müller, E. Kremers.

Soviet Union: Rudakov, Dzodzuashvili, Khurtsilava, Kaplychniy, Istomin, Kolotov, Troshkin, Konkov, Baidachny (Kozynkevych 66), Banishevski (Dolmatov 46), Onyshchenko.

ABOVE: Gerd Müller's international strike-rate was better than one goal per game; in competitive matches, it was 40 goals in 31, and he netted twice in the UEFA EURO 72 final.

UEFA EUROPEAN FOOTBALL CHAMPIONSHIP 1974–76

The 1972 tournament may have featured an outstanding team in West Germany, but the 1976 event went three better, producing no fewer than four superbly competitive sides.

Hosts Yugoslavia finished fourth after losing the third-place play-off to the Netherlands, but there was no embarrassment in that. These stand as probably the most thrilling finals of the tournament's "first" generation and the final between Czechoslovakia and holders West Germany provided a dramatic climax.

Once again the formula provided for a first round of eight mini-league groups of four nations apiece. The Czechoslovaks made an unpromising start by losing 3–0 to England at Wembley. Three goals in the last 18 minutes from Mick Channon and Colin Bell (two) consigned them to a defeat which gave no hint of the remarkable revival that was to come.

Later, England emphatically beat Cyprus 5–0, with Malcolm MacDonald scoring all five goals before they lost their grip on group one and Czechoslovakia progressed instead.

Wales were the surprising winners of group two, while Yugoslavia, Spain, the Soviet Union, Belgium, West Germany and the Netherlands (who edged out Italy) all reached the quarter-finals.

The pattern of excitement at the finals in Yugoslavia was set when Czechoslovakia defeated the Netherlands 3–1 after extra time in the first semi-final. The Dutch succumbed after Welsh referee Clive Thomas sent off midfielders Johan Neeskens and Wim Van Hanegem.

Next it was West Germany's turn to require extra time as they hit back from 2–0 down to beat hosts Yugoslavia 4–2. The Germans had found a new Müller – Dieter Müller from Cologne. He scored a hat-trick against the Yugoslavs and then one more to inspire a fightback in the final against Czechoslovakia after Germany had gone two-down in 25 minutes.

One minute remained in normal time when Bernd Hölzenbein equalised to make it 2–2 and send the game into extra time. No more goals followed and the Czechoslovaks won the penalty shootout 5–3, climaxed by a cheeky chip from Antonín Panenka. That style of spot kick would forever bear his name.

ABOVE: The moment a new word entered the football lexicon. Antonin Panenka chips his penalty past Sepp Maier's dive, the "Panenka" helping Czechoslovakia win the 1976 final against West Germany.

FOR THE RECORD

SEMI-FINALS
CZECHOSLOVAKIA	3–1	Netherlands (AET)
WEST GERMANY	4–2	Yugoslavia (AET)

THIRD-PLACE PLAY-OFF
NETHERLANDS	3–2	Yugoslavia (AET)

FINAL (STADION CRVENA ZVEZDA, BELGRADE)
CZECHOSLOVAKIA 2–2 West Germany (AET)

Švehlík 8	D Müller 28
Dobiaš 25	Hölzenbein 89

(Czechoslovakia won 5–3 on pens, after extra time)

HT: 2–1
90 min: 2–2
ATT: 33,000
Ref: Gonella (Italy)

Czechoslovakia: Viktor, Pivarník, Ondruš, Čapkovič, Gögh, Dobiaš (Veselý 109), Panenka, Móder, Masný, Švehlík, Nehoda (Biroš 80).

West Germany: Maier, Vogts, Beckenbauer, Schwarzenbeck, Dietz, Wimmer (Flohe 46), Bonhof, Beer (Bongartz 80), Hoeness, D. Müller, Hölzenbein.

UEFA EUROPEAN FOOTBALL CHAMPIONSHIP 1978–80

The 1980 finals marked the start of an expansive new era. Such was the popularity of the tournament, that UEFA decided to increase the scope of the finals to take in eight countries – split into two groups of four with the group-winners meeting in the final.

ABOVE: Horst Hrubesch scored twice in the 1980 final against Belgium, emulating compatriot Gerd Müller as a two-goal scorer in the final of the UEFA European Football Championship.

The expansion of the finals meant that the hosts – in this case Italy (who would become the first nation to host the tournament twice) – had to be designated well in advance and their "reward" was to get a bye straight to the finals.

This meant a qualifying tournament featuring 31 teams, arranged in three groups of five and four groups of four. The group winners progressed to expanded, eight-team finals.

The teams were sorted into two mini-leagues, and goals were at a premium, with 12 group matches seeing the net found only 22 times. In group two England and Italy both disappointed. The Italians' failure to beat Belgium in their concluding game meant the outsiders advanced to the final instead of the hosts.

Group one saw West Germany establish themselves as tournament favourites as they topped the table courtesy of a 1–0 revenge victory over Czechoslovakia, a 3–2 win over the Netherlands – when the international game "discovered" an inspirational young midfielder named Bernd Schuster – and a goalless draw with Greece.

As group runners-up Italy went into the third-place play-off match, but lost it 9–8 in a penalty shootout to Czechoslovakia following a 1–1 draw. It was the last occasion the play-off match was contested and semi-finals were re-introduced from 1984.

West Germany's triumph in the final owed much to a new hero from Bayern Munich, Karl-Heinz Rummenigge. He provided the cross from which Horst Hrubesch headed a last-minute winning goal against Belgium. Earlier, the Germans had taken the lead through Hrubesch in the tenth minute, only for Belgium to equalise with a second-half Rene Vandereycken penalty.

UEFA EUROPEAN FOOTBALL CHAMPIONSHIP 1982–84

In 1984, Michel Platini's magnificent Frenchmen proved the undisputed cream of the continent as they swept all before them to win the ultimate prize in the redeveloped Parc des Princes in Paris.

France had qualified directly for the finals as tournament hosts, while the other qualifiers were the winners of the mini-leagues that comprised four groups of five teams and three groups of four.

The changing balance of the international game was reflected in the make-up of the finals. France's brilliance emanated from the midfield foundation Luis Fernández, Jean Tigana and Alain Giresse provided for the all-round attacking genius of skipper Platini.

Denmark's presence in the finals was another gesture towards a new balance of power within Europe. Unfortunately, injury hampered their prospects in the finals in which they opened with a 1–0 defeat by France, during which their star player Allan Simonsen broke a leg.

Platini scored the match-winning goal – the first of his nine in five games. He then netted hat-tricks against both Belgium and Yugoslavia, scored the last-minute of extra-time winner in the semi-final against Portugal, and the first goal of the final itself against Spain.

The Spaniards misfired in draws against Romania and Portugal but upset West Germany 1–0 in their final group game to reach the last four. Miguel Muñoz's men beat Denmark in a penalty shoot-out in their semi-final before their luck ran out in the final.

A rare slip by goalkeeper-captain Luis Arconada allowed Platini's drive from a free-kick to spin over the goal-line. France even overcame the sending off of defender Yvon Le Roux before Bruno Bellone added a 90th-minute goal to seal a historic victory.

FOR THE RECORD

GROUP 1

		P	W	D	L	F	A	Pts
1	France	3	3	0	0	9	2	6
2	Denmark	3	2	0	1	8	3	4
3	Belgium	3	1	0	2	4	8	2
4	Yugoslavia	3	0	0	3	2	10	0

GROUP 2

		P	W	D	L	F	A	Pts
1	Spain	3	1	2	0	3	2	4
2	Portugal	3	1	2	0	2	1	4
3	West Germany	3	1	1	2	2	2	3
4	Romania	3	0	1	2	2	4	1

SEMI-FINALS

FRANCE	3–2	Portugal (AET)
SPAIN	1–1	Denmark (AET)

(Spain won 5–4 on pens, after extra time)

FINAL (PARC DES PRINCES, PARIS)

FRANCE	2–0	Spain

Platini 56
Bellone 90

HT: 0–0
Att: 47,368
Ref: Christov (Czechoslovakia)

France: Bats, Battiston (Amoros 73), *Le Roux, Bossis, Domergue, Fernandez, Giresse, Tigana, Platini, Lacombe (Genghini 80), Bellone.
*Le Roux sent off, 85min.

Spain: Arconada, Urquiaga, Salva (Roberto 85), Gallego, Señor, Francisco, Victor, Camacho, Julio Alberto (Sarabia 75), Santillana, Carrasco.

ABOVE: Two Portugal defenders and goalkeeper Bento cannot stop Michel Platini's semi-final match-winner in the last minute of extra-time in Marseille.

UEFA EUROPEAN FOOTBALL CHAMPIONSHIP 1986–88

The Netherlands had found national team success elusive, but after finishing as FIFA World Cup runners-up in 1974 and 1978, the Dutch finally secured the major prize their international pre-eminence had long since earned. Their victory over the Soviet Union in Munich's Olympiastadion vindicated their progressive football approach.

The format remained unchanged. A qualifying section of mini-leagues was climaxed by two four-team groups in the finals, two direct elimination semi-finals and then the final itself.

Italy, the Soviet Union, England and the Netherlands swept all before them in their respective qualifying groups. Spain, Denmark and the Republic of Ireland – qualifying for a major finals for the first time – all had to scrap.

England flew to the finals with the best record of any of the qualifiers, having won five and drawn one of their matches, scoring 19 goals and conceding just one. Yet they lost all three group matches. A 1–0 setback against the Irish newcomers was followed by devastating defeats to the Netherlands, for whom Marco van Basten scored a hat-trick, and the Soviet Union.

West Germany topped the other group, ahead of Italy, and led the Netherlands in their semi-final after a Lothar Matthäus penalty. However, the Dutch hit back immediately from a Ronald Koeman spot kick before van Basten snatched a late winner. The other semi-final saw the Soviet Union extend their fine tournament record with a 2–0 victory over Italy.

In the final, the Netherlands met a Soviet side missing the significant defensive presence of Oleh Kuznetsov through suspension. Even Kuznetsov, however, would not have been able to withstand the attacking flair of Dutch skipper Ruud Gullit and van Basten.

Gullit scored the first goal and Van Basten the second – volleying home from Arnold Mühren's cross – one of the greatest individual goals scored in a major final. The Soviet Union had a chance to get back into the game as Hans van Breukelen conceded a penalty, but saved Igor Belanov's kick.

FOR THE RECORD

GROUP 1

		P	W	D	L	F	A	Pts
1	West Germany	3	2	1	0	5	1	5
2	Italy	3	2	1	0	4	1	5
3	Spain	3	1	0	2	3	5	2
4	Denmark	3	0	0	3	2	7	0

GROUP 2

		P	W	D	L	F	A	Pts
1	Soviet Union	3	2	1	0	5	2	5
2	Netherlands	3	2	0	1	4	2	4
3	Republic of Ireland	3	1	1	1	2	2	3
4	England	3	0	0	3	2	7	0

SEMI-FINALS
NETHERLANDS   2–1   West Germany
SOVIET UNION   2–0   Italy

FINAL (OLYMPIASTADION, MUNICH)
NETHERLANDS   2–0   Soviet Union
Gullit 33
Van Basten 54

HT: 1–0
Att: 72,300
Ref: Vautrot (France)

Netherlands: van Breukelen, van Aerle, R. Koeman, Rijkaard, van Tiggelen, Vanenburg, Wouters, E. Koeman, Mühren, Gullit, van Basten.

Soviet Union: Dasayev, Khidiyatulin, Demianenko, Lytovchenko, Aleinikov, Zavarov, Belanov, Mykhailychenko, Gotsmanov (Baltacha 68), Rats, Protasov (Pasulko 71).

BELOW: Marco van Basten's stunning volley early in the second half sealed the Netherlands' 2–0 victory in the final against the Soviet Union.

UEFA EUROPEAN FOOTBALL CHAMPIONSHIP 1990–92

Denmark came from nowhere to win the tournament for the first time after, remarkably, overcoming first the Netherlands in the semi-finals and then Germany, in their first post-unification tournament, in the final.

ABOVE: Denmark's Kim Vilfort (lying on his back) is mobbed by team-mates – including the scorer of the opener, John Jensen, 7 – after firing home the second goal of the final to end German hopes.

Political upheavals had caused major disruption since the previous tournament with the disappearance of the former East Germany and the break-up of both the Soviet Union and Yugoslavia.

The latter had been one of the more outstanding qualifiers, but the onset of domestic conflict led UEFA to exclude them on security grounds. Denmark, runners-up in the Yugoslavs' qualifying group, were called up at two weeks' notice. Coach Richard Møller Nielsen heard the news while he was in the middle of decorating his kitchen.

Sweden provided a suitably peaceable venue. The hosts, in the finals for the first time, topped Group A after a wonderful goal from Tomas Brolin earned a 2–1 victory over a disappointing England in the last round of group matches. Denmark sneaked into the semi-finals as runners-up after a similar win over a French side managed by old hero Michel Platini.

In Group B, the Netherlands and Germany possessed too much firepower and experience for newcomers Scotland and the Commonwealth of Independent States, as the transitional replacement for the Soviet Union was known.

The semi-finals produced great entertainment. The Dutch – imperious in qualifying – succumbed against Denmark, being held 2–2 and losing 5–4 on penalties. Remarkably, the decisive penalty miss came courtesy of Marco van Basten, the hero four years earlier.

Brolin scored again for Sweden in the other semi-final, but this time in vain in a 3–2 defeat by Germany.

The Germans were runaway favourites to win the final in Gothenburg. But Denmark – from goalkeeper Peter Schmeichel, skipper and centre-back Lars Olsen, midfielder Kim Vilfort and forward Brian Laudrup – had not read the script. Goals from John Jensen and Vilfort produced one of the greatest shocks in the competition's history.

UEFA EUROPEAN FOOTBALL CHAMPIONSHIP 1994–96

The 1996 finals took the UEFA European Football Championship to a new level. Entry doubled to 16 finalists in four groups in what turned out to be the most exciting football extravaganza in England since their 1966 FIFA World Cup triumph.

England drew 1–1 against Switzerland in the opening match before pulling off a dramatic 2–0 victory over old rivals Scotland (with goals from Alan Shearer and Paul Gascoigne) and a high-class 4–1 defeat of the Netherlands.

France topped Group B, ahead of Spain but Denmark's reign as European champions ended abruptly when Croatia and Portugal pipped them in Group D. Italy were eliminated from Group C, from which both Germany and the Czech Republic qualified.

Penalties in the quarter-finals proved decisive for both England (against Spain) and France (against the Netherlands). The Czechs beat Portugal 1–0, while Germany triumphed 2–1 over Croatia.

Shootouts also resolved both semi-finals. The Czechs pipped France after a 0–0 draw. By contrast England versus Germany provided a night of exciting intensity at Wembley.

England led through a Shearer header with Germany levelling through Stefan Kuntz. The drama continued into golden goal extra time, before a penalty shootout was needed. Eventually, England defender Gareth Southgate saw his spot kick beaten away by German keeper Andreas Köpke. Andreas Möller then fired home the decisive penalty to take Germany into the final.

Now the sudden-death golden goal proved decisive. Patrik Berger fired the Czechs ahead from a penalty to prompt German coach Berti Vogts into sending on substitute striker Oliver Bierhoff. Within five minutes, Bierhoff had headed the Germans level then, early in extra time, he shot the most golden of goals.

FOR THE RECORD

GROUP A

		P	W	D	L	F	A	Pts
1	England	3	2	1	0	7	2	7
2	Netherlands	3	1	1	1	3	4	4
3	Scotland	3	1	1	1	1	2	4
4	Switzerland	3	0	1	2	1	4	1

GROUP B

		P	W	D	L	F	A	Pts
1	France	3	2	1	0	5	2	7
2	Spain	3	1	2	0	4	3	5
3	Bulgaria	3	1	1	1	3	4	4
4	Romania	3	0	0	3	1	4	0

GROUP C

		P	W	D	L	F	A	Pts
1	Germany	3	2	1	0	5	0	7
2	Czech Republic	3	1	1	1	5	6	4
3	Italy	3	1	1	1	3	3	4
4	Russia	3	0	1	2	4	8	1

GROUP D

		P	W	D	L	F	A	Pts
1	Portugal	3	2	1	0	5	2	7
2	Croatia	3	2	0	1	4	3	6
3	Denmark	3	1	1	1	4	4	4
4	Turkey	3	0	0	3	0	5	0

QUARTER-FINALS

ENGLAND 0–0 Sweden (AET)
(England won 4–2 on pens, after extra time)
FRANCE 2–2 Netherlands (AET)
(France won 5–4 on pens, after extra time)
GERMANY 2–1 Croatia
CZECH REPUBLIC 1–0 Portugal

SEMI-FINALS

CZECH REPUBLIC 0–0 France (AET)
(Czech Republic won 6–5 on pens, after extra time)
GERMANY 1–1 England (AET)
(Germany win 6–5 on pens, after extra time)

FINAL (WEMBLEY STADIUM, LONDON)

GERMANY 2–1 Czech Republic (AET)
Bierhoff 73, 95   *Berger 59 pen*
(Germany won on golden goal in extra time)

HT: 0–0
90 min: 1–1
Att: 76,000
Ref: Pairetto (Italy)

Germany: Köpke, Babbel, Sammer, Helmer, Strunz, Hässler, Eilts (Bode 46), Scholl (Bierhoff 69), Ziege, Klinsmann, Kuntz.

Czech Republic: Kouba, Horňák, Rada, Kadlec, Suchopárek, Poborský (Šmicer 88), Nedvěd, Bejbl, Berger, Němec, Kuka.

ABOVE: England's second goal, scored spectacularly by Paul Gascoigne, finally saw off Scotland in a thrilling and tension-filled Group A encounter at Wembley.

UEFA EUROPEAN FOOTBALL CHAMPIONSHIP 1998–2000

The first finals of the new millennium were co-hosted for the first time, by Belgium and the Netherlands, while France duly regained the crown they had won in 1984, following a thrilling 2–1 golden-goal victory over an Italian team who delighted their own fans by reaching the final.

FOR THE RECORD

GROUP A

		P	W	D	L	F	A	Pts
1	Portugal	3	3	0	0	7	2	9
2	Romania	3	1	1	1	4	4	4
3	England	3	1	0	2	5	6	3
4	Germany	3	0	1	2	1	5	1

GROUP B

		P	W	D	L	F	A	Pts
1	Italy	3	2	1	0	6	2	7
2	Turkey	3	1	2	0	3	2	5
3	Belgium	3	1	1	1	2	5	4
4	Sweden	3	0	1	2	2	4	1

GROUP C

		P	W	D	L	F	A	Pts
1	Spain	3	2	0	1	6	5	6
2	Yugoslavia	3	1	1	1	7	7	4
3	Norway	3	1	1	1	1	1	3
4	Slovenia	3	0	2	1	4	5	2

GROUP D

		P	W	D	L	F	A	Pts
1	Netherlands	3	3	0	0	7	2	9
2	France	3	2	0	1	7	4	6
3	Czech Republic	3	1	0	2	3	3	3
4	Denmark	3	0	0	3	0	8	0

QUARTER-FINALS

PORTUGAL	2–0	Turkey
ITALY	2–0	Romania
FRANCE	2–1	Spain
NETHERLANDS	6–1	Yugoslavia

SEMI-FINALS

FRANCE	2–1	Portugal (AET)

(France won on golden goal in extra time)

ITALY	0–0	Netherlands (AET)

(Italy won 3–1 on pens, after extra time)

FINAL (FEIJENOORD STADION, ROTTERDAM)

FRANCE	2–1	Italy (AET)
Wiltord 90		*Delvecchio 56*
Trezeguet 103		

(France won on golden goal in extra time)

HT: 0–0
90 min: 1–1
Att: 55,000
Ref: Frisk (Sweden)

France: Barthez, Thuram, Blanc, Desailly, Lizarazu (Pires 86), Djorkaeff (Trezeguet 76), Vieira, Deschamps, Dugarry (Wiltord 58), Zidane, Henry.

Italy: Toldo, Cannavaro, Nesta, Iuliano, Pessotto, Di Biagio (Ambrosini 66), Albertini, Fiore (Del Piero 53), Maldini, Totti, Delvecchio (Montella 86).

These finals provided thrill-a-minute football that will live long in the memory of all who were there.

The final was one such occasion. Italy, in defiance of their defensive traditions, traded lightning raids blow for blow with the FIFA World Cup holders in a goalless first half and went ahead through Marco Delvecchio 11 minutes into the second half.

Italy were almost reaching out for the trophy when their defence could not clear one last attack and substitute Sylvain Wiltord equalised. Psychologically undermined, the *Azzurri* conceded a golden goal winner to David Trezeguet in the 103rd minute.

England had a disappointing tournament, falling by the wayside along with Germany in the same group.

Against expectations, the qualifiers from the group were a disciplined Romania and an inspired Portugal, who went on to reach the semi-finals before losing dramatically to France, on a golden-goal penalty converted by a nerveless Zinedine Zidane.

The second semi-final was decided by the only penalty shootout of the event, the Netherlands falling 3–1 to Italy after a 0–0 extra time draw. The cliché about a team "paying the penalty" was never more apt. The Netherlands' Frank de Boer and Kluivert not only both missed penalties for the Dutch in normal time but De Boer, Jaap Stam and Paul Bosvelt also failed in the shootout. Italy battled through despite playing all but the first half-hour with only ten men after Gianluca Zambrotta was sent off.

ABOVE: David Trezeguet (20) scores the golden goal winner as France defeat Italy 2–1 to complete a stunning comeback. They equalised, through Sylvain Wiltord, three minutes into second-half added time.

UEFA EUROPEAN FOOTBALL CHAMPIONSHIP 2002-04

A second-half goal from striker Angelos Charisteas in Lisbon's Estádio da Luz punctured the Portuguese hosts' euphoria and handed rank outsiders Greece their first major title. The Greeks thus became the first nation to beat both the hosts and holders (France) in the same tournament. Greece's triumph was down to fitness, organisation and the pragmatic management of veteran German Otto Rehhagel.

FOR THE RECORD

GROUP A

		P	W	D	L	F	A	Pts
1	Portugal	3	2	0	1	4	2	6
2	Greece	3	1	1	1	4	4	4
3	Spain	3	1	1	1	2	2	4
4	Russia	3	1	0	2	2	4	1

GROUP B

		P	W	D	L	F	A	Pts
1	France	3	2	1	0	7	4	7
2	England	3	2	0	1	8	4	6
3	Croatia	3	0	2	1	4	6	4
4	Switzerland	3	0	1	2	1	6	1

GROUP C

		P	W	D	L	F	A	Pts
1	Sweden	3	1	2	0	8	3	5
2	Denmark	3	1	2	0	4	2	5
3	Italy	3	1	2	0	3	2	5
4	Bulgaria	3	0	0	3	1	9	0

GROUP D

		P	W	D	L	F	A	Pts
1	Czech Republic	3	3	0	0	7	4	9
2	Netherlands	3	1	1	1	6	4	6
3	Germany	3	0	2	1	2	3	2
4	Latvia	3	0	1	2	1	5	1

QUARTER-FINALS

PORTUGAL	2–2	England (AET)

(Portugal won 6–5 on pens, after extra time)

NETHERLANDS	0–0	Sweden (AET)

(Netherlands won 5–4 on pens, after extra time)

GREECE	1–0	France
CZECH REPUBLIC	3–0	Denmark

SEMI-FINALS

PORTUGAL	2–1	Netherlands
GREECE	1–0	Czech Republic (AET)

(Greece won on silver goal, after extra time)

FINAL (BENFICA, LISBON)

GREECE	1–0	Portugal

Charisteas 57

HT: 0–0
Att: 62,865
Ref: Merk (Germany)

Greece: Nikopolidis, Seitaridis, Dellas, Kapsis, Fyssas, Giannakopoulos (Venetidis 76), Basinas, Zagorakis, Katsouranis, Charisteas, Vryzas (Papadopoulos 81).

Portugal: Ricardo, Miguel (Ferreira 43), Ricardo Carvalho, Jorge Andrade, Nuno Valente (Costinha (Rui Costa 60), Maniche, Figo, Deco, Cristiano Ronaldo, Pauleta (Nuno Gomes 74).

At the start of the finals Greece had not figured among the nations with title hopes. The so-called "Big Five" were the biggest let-downs. Germany, Italy and Spain all crashed in the first round and England and France fell in the quarter-finals, along with Denmark and Sweden. A tenacious Netherlands side reached the semi-finals before falling to Portugal.

The ideal final in prospect would have matched Portuguese against Czech Republic but the Greeks had other ideas, beating the Czechs on the silver-goal rule and then tarnishing the dreams of Portugal's so-called golden generation in the final.

So the finals ended as they had begun with a Greek defeat of Portugal. The only difference was the scoreline. The opening match in Oporto in Group A had seen Portugal lose 2–1 to Rehhagel's Greek surprise package.

The hosts managed to recover their self-belief with a 2–0 victory over Russia to top their group ahead of Greece, who suffered their only defeat of the finals, losing 2–1 to the already eliminated Russians.

France and England emerged from Group B in that order with four-goal Wayne Rooney making an explosive impact at his first senior tournament. But he injured a foot early in

ABOVE: Greece's defeat of Portugal in the final – they also beat the hosts in a group match – was one of the most surprising results in UEFA European Football Championship history.

the quarter-final against Portugal, who won 6–5 on penalties.

France lost their grip on the title when they slipped up 1–0 in their own quarter-final against the Greeks. Charisteas scored the lone goal ... as he would against Portugal in the final.

UEFA EUROPEAN FOOTBALL CHAMPIONSHIP 2006–08

Spain, for so many years Europe's most frustrating national team, finally turned a long corner when they triumphed in Vienna. In winning the 2008 crown by defeating Germany 1–0 in the final, they made amends for years of not realising their potential at FIFA World Cups and UEFA European Championships.

La Roja were worthy winners of their first major prize since 1964. They won every one their six games – albeit the quarter-final against Italy thanks to two fine penalty saves from Iker Casillas – and had enough in hand to overcome Germany in the final.

A first-half goal from Fernando Torres brought Spain a second European title a massive 44 years after their one and only, and rewarded their first appearance in a final since defeat by hosts France in 1984.

Overall UEFA EURO 2008 generated a lot of football fun. It had some excellent football, gripping drama plus some outstanding goals and superb saves. The only disappointment for local fans was that neither of the co-hosts, Austria or Switzerland, progressed beyond the group stage.

Portugal topped Group A ahead of Turkey, while Croatia started impressively by winning all three games in Group B, including a 2–1 victory over eventual runners-up Germany. Group C was the most dramatic, with the Netherlands magnificent and Italy fighting back in steely fashion after losing 3–0 against the Dutch in the first match.

Spain were commanding winners of Group D ahead of Russia, then were shootout winners in the quarter-finals against Italy. A shootout also saw Turkey edge out Croatia before their luck ran out in the semi-finals against Germany.

FOR THE RECORD

GROUP A

		P	W	D	L	F	A	Pts
1	Portugal	3	2	0	1	5	3	6
2	Turkey	3	2	0	1	5	5	6
3	Czech Republic	3	1	0	2	4	6	3
4	Switzerland	3	1	0	2	3	3	3

GROUP B

		P	W	D	L	F	A	Pts
1	Croatia	3	3	0	0	4	1	9
2	Germany	3	2	0	1	4	2	6
3	Austria	3	0	1	2	1	3	1
4	Poland	3	0	1	2	1	4	1

GROUP C

		P	W	D	L	F	A	Pts
1	Netherlands	3	3	0	0	9	1	9
2	Italy	3	1	1	1	3	4	4
3	Romania	3	0	2	1	1	3	2
4	France	3	0	1	2	1	6	1

GROUP D

		P	W	D	L	F	A	Pts
1	Spain	3	3	0	0	8	3	9
2	Russia	3	2	0	1	4	4	6
3	Sweden	3	1	0	2	3	4	3
4	Greece	3	0	0	3	1	5	0

QUARTER-FINALS
GERMANY	3–2	Portugal
TURKEY	1–1	Croatia (AET)

(Turkey won 3–1 on pens, after extra time)

RUSSIA	3–1	Netherlands
SPAIN	0–0	Italy (AET)

(Spain won 4–2 on pens, after extra time)

SEMI-FINALS
GERMANY	3–2	Turkey
SPAIN	3–0	Russia

FINAL (ERNST-HAPPEL-STADION, VIENNA)
SPAIN	1–0	Germany

Torres 33

HT: 1–0
Att: 51,428
Ref: Rosetti (Italy)

Spain: Casillas, Sergio Ramos, Puyol, Marchena, Capdevila, Senna, Iniesta, Xavi, Fàbregas (Xabi Alonso 63), David Silva (Santi 66), Torres (Güiza 78).

Germany: Lehmann, Friedrich, Mertesacker, Metzelder, Lahm (Jansen 46), Frings, Hitzlsperger (Kuranyi 58), Schweinsteiger, Ballack, Podolski, Klose (Gomez 79).

ABOVE: Fernando Torres shoots past German goalkeeper Jens Lehmann for the only goal of the 2008 UEFA European Football Championship final to give Spain their first major tournament for 44 years.

UEFA EUROPEAN FOOTBALL CHAMPIONSHIP 2010–12 •✶

Poland and Ukraine co-hosted the first UEFA European Football Championship to be staged in Eastern Europe. Defending champions Spain fashioned football history to retain the trophy by crushing Italy 4–0 in the final in Kyiv.

ABOVE: Andrea Pirlo weaved his magic in Italy's wins against England, above, and Germany, but the *Azzurri* were no match for Spain, who won by a record margin in a UEFA European Football Championship final.

Victory established Spain, also FIFA World Cup-holders, as the only nation ever to raise three major trophies in a row and the only country ever to retain the European title. Their 4–0 defeat of Italy was also the biggest margin of victory in the final in the tournament's 52-year history.

Goals from David Silva and Jordi Alba in the first half, then from substitutes Fernando Torres and Juan Mata in the second also provided father-figure Vicente del Bosque a personal footnote in history: he was the first coach to win the FIFA World Cup, UEFA European Football Championship and UEFA Champions League.

Spain's magnificence enthralled fans and experts alike, though it

was disappointing that both co-hosts, Poland and Ukraine, failed to progress beyond the group stage.

Spain had opened up in Group C, despite missing injured top scorer David Villa, with a 1–1 draw against Italy. Fernando Torres scored twice in a 4–0 win over the Republic of Ireland before a late strike from substitute Jesus Navas saw off Croatia. Italy followed Spain through as runners-up.

England's campaign, under newly arrived manager Roy Hodgson, ended in a defeat on penalties to Italy in the quarter-finals. The *Azzurri* then beat Germany 2–1 in the semi-finals with an inspirational display from veteran schemer Andrea Pirlo.

France won their second UEFA European Football Championship in the Netherlands in 2000 when David Trezeguet, shirtless, scored the "golden goal" winner in the final against Italy. He is hugging the man who scored the stoppage-time equaliser, Sylvain Wiltord (15).

Chapter 5
UEFA European Football Championship Records

FRANCE WILL SET A RECORD IN 2016 WHEN THEY BECOME THE FIRST NATION TO HOST THE UEFA EUROPEAN FOOTBALL CHAMPIONSHIP FINALS ON THREE OCCASIONS. THEY HOPE TO EQUAL ANOTHER RECORD ON THE STADE DE FRANCE PITCH ON 10 JULY BECAUSE, IF *LES BLEUS* WIN THE FINAL, THEY WILL JOIN GERMANY AND SPAIN AS THREE-TIME WINNERS. WITH EXTRA ROUNDS OF GAMES IN THE EXPANDED 24-TEAM UEFA EURO 2016, IT IS QUITE POSSIBLE THAT SWEDISH SUPERSTAR ZLATAN IBRAHIMOVIĆ WILL SCORE THE FOUR GOALS HE NEEDS TO MAKE HIM THE ALL-TIME LEADING MARKSMAN IN UEFA EUROPEAN FOOTBALL CHAMPIONSHIP HISTORY.

Anyone looking for omens when searching for the winners of UEFA EURO 2016 will remember that the last time France were champions was in 1984, and that was also the last time the country played host to the UEFA European Football Championship. Their talisman in 1984, Michel Platini, still holds the record for the most goals in a single tournament, with nine, including two hat-tricks, and he also scored in all five matches *Les Bleus* played.

TEAM RECORDS

MOST TITLES

3 ...... Germany (1972, 1980, 1996)
Spain (1964, 2008, 2012)
2 ...... France (1984, 2000)
1 ...... Czechoslovakia (1976)
Denmark (1992)
Greece (2004)
Italy (1968)
Netherlands (1988)
Soviet Union (1960)

ABOVE: Jürgen Klinsmann (18) and Stefan Kuntz (11) celebrate Oliver Bierhoff's winning goal in the 1996 UEFA European Football Championship final and Germany become the EURO's first triple champions.

GERMANY OUT IN FRONT

Germany's record of consistency in the tournament is all the more remarkable considering that they did not enter the first two competitions (in 1958–60 and 1962–64). They have played more finals games (43), have won more matches (23) and scored more goals (65) than any other nation. They have also conceded more goals than anyone else (45).

PORTUGAL ALL AT SEA

Portugal in 2004 were the first host nation to reach the final since France had achieved the same feat 20 years earlier. They are also the only host nation to have lost in a final, by 1–0 to Greece in Lisbon.

DUTCH DELIGHT

The first-ever UEFA EURO qualifying play-off was held on 13 December 1995, in Liverpool. The Netherlands beat the Republic of Ireland 2–0 to clinch their place at UEFA EURO 96. Patrick Kluivert scored both goals.

MOST APPEARANCES IN FINALS

11 .... West Germany/Germany
10 .... Russia/Soviet Union/CIS
9 ...... Spain
Netherlands
8 ...... Czech Republic/
Czechoslovakia
Denmark
England
France
Italy
6 ...... Portugal

DOUBLE WINNERS

Three nations have shared the glory of being reigning European and world champions simultaneously. West Germany won their first European title in 1972 and followed up by winning the FIFA World Cup two years later; France reversed the order, winning the FIFA World Cup in 1998 and adding the European crown in 2000; then Spain won two European titles in 2008 and 2012 either side of their FIFA World Cup success in 2010.

EARLY OPENING IN IRELAND

The first qualifying round tie in the UEFA European Nations' Cup, as the competition was then known, was played on 5 April 1959, when the Republic of Ireland beat Czechoslovakia 2–0 in Dublin. As 17 teams entered the inaugural tournament, the total had to be reduced to 16 for the first round. The Czechs went through 4–2 on aggregate, winning 4–0 in Bratislava. France, however, had already beaten Greece 8–2 on aggregate in the first round.

FAROE ISLANDS' WINNING START

The Faroe Islands entered the qualifiers for the first time in 1992 – and began with a shock 1–0 defeat of Austria at Landskrona, Sweden. Torkil Nielsen scored the only goal in the 61st minute. Austria coach Josef Hickersberger was sacked after the defeat. That was the Faroe Islands' only win and they finished bottom of a group also featuring Yugoslavia, Denmark and Northern Ireland.

ABOVE: Spain joined France and West Germany – losing finalists in 2008 (above) – as the only nations to simultaneously be European and World champions.

BIGGEST WIN IN QUALIFYING

Germany's 13–0 win in San Marino on 6 September 2006 was the biggest victory margin in UEFA EURO qualifying history. Lukas Podolski (four), Miroslav Klose (two), Bastian Schweinsteiger (two), Thomas Hitzlsperger (two), Michael Ballack, Manuel Friedrich and Bernd Schneider scored the goals. The previous biggest win had been Spain's 12–1 rout of Malta in 1983.

EAST AND WEST DIVIDE

East and West Germany were originally drawn to face each other in the qualifying groups for UEFA EURO 1992. But the country was officially re-unified in October 1990. So a unified Germany duly competed in international competition for the first time since the 1938 FIFA World Cup.

FRENCH SLIP-UP

France are the only European champions who have failed to qualify to defend their title since the group stage was added in 1980. The 1984 holders finished third in their group, behind the Soviet Union and East Germany, so they stayed home for UEFA EURO 1988.

THE PERFECT TEN

England were the only team to win all their ten qualifying matches en route to the 2016 finals. They scored 31 goals and conceded three for a tournament-best goal difference of plus-28. Captain Wayne Rooney was their seven-goal top scorer, including four penalties – more spot kicks than any other player in the qualifiers.

ABOVE: Wayne Rooney became England's all-time leading goalscorer in EURO 2016 qualifying.

FINALS HOSTS

1960	France
1964	Spain
1968	Italy
1972	Belgium
1976	Yugoslavia
1980	Italy
1984	France
1988	West Germany
1992	Sweden
1996	England
2000	Netherlands and Belgium
2004	Portugal
2008	Austria and Switzerland
2012	Poland and Ukraine

In total:

2 ...... Belgium (1972, 2000 with The Netherlands), France (1960, 1984), Italy (1968, 1980)

1 ...... Austria (2008 with Switzerland), England (1996), West Germany (1988), The Netherlands (2000 with Belgium), Poland (2012 with Ukraine), Portugal (2004), Spain (1964), Sweden (1992), Switzerland (2008 with Austria), Ukraine (2012 with Poland), Yugoslavia (1976)

PLAYER RECORDS

FINALS LEADING APPEARANCES

16.... Lilian Thuram (France)
       Edwin van der Sar
       (Netherlands)
14.... Iker Casillas (Spain)
       Philipp Lahm (Germany)
       Luís Figo (Portugal)
       Nuno Gomes (Portugal)
       Karel Poborský (Czech
              Republic)
       Cristiano Ronaldo (Portugal)
       Zinedine Zidane (France)

STAYING POWER

Eight players have appeared in four finals tournaments:

Lothar Matthäus	(West Germany/Germany)	1980, 1984, 1988, 2000
Peter Schmeichel	(Denmark)	1988, 1992, 1996, 2000
Aron Winter	(Netherlands)	1988, 1992, 1996, 2000
Alessandro del Piero	(Italy)	1996, 2000, 2004, 2008
Edwin van der Sar	(Netherlands)	1996, 2000, 2004, 2008
Lilian Thuram	(France)	1996, 2000, 2004, 2008
Olof Mellberg	(Sweden)	2000, 2004, 2008, 2012
Iker Casillas	(Spain)	2000, 2004, 2008, 2012

GOLDEN BOY BIERHOFF

Germany's Oliver Bierhoff scored the first golden goal in the tournament's history when he hit the winner against the Czech Republic in the UEFA EURO 96 final at Wembley. The golden goal rule meant that the first team to score in extra time won the match. UEFA later introduced a silver goal that allowed the match to proceed to its next timed break. In the UEFA EURO 2004 semi-finals Greece beat the Czech Republic thanks to a silver goal from Trainos Dellas.

SUPERMAC'S RECORD

Malcolm Macdonald netted all five goals in England's 5–0 qualifying defeat of Cyprus on 16 April 1975. He equalled England's scoring record, first set by Howard Vaughton in 1882. Tibor Nylasi (Hungary v Luxembourg, 19 October 1975) and Marco Van Basten (Netherlands v Malta, 19 December 1990), also scored five in qualifiers.

ABOVE: Oliver Bierhoff scored the first golden goal a EURO finals. He was the third player – all German – to have netted a double in the final itself, joining Gerd Müller and Horst Hrubesch.

DEFENSIVE SLIPS

Glen Johnson became only the fifth man to score an own goal at a UEFA European Football Championship finals, when the England right-back put through his own net against Sweden in their UEFA EURO 2012 first-round clash. The earlier unfortunates were Czechoslovakia's Anton Ondruš in 1976, Bulgaria's Luboslav Penev in 1996, Yugoslavia's Dejan Govedarica in 2000 and Portugal's Jorge Andrade in 2004.

ALL-TIME FINALS TOP SCORERS

9 ...... Michel Platini (France)
7 ...... Alan Shearer (England)
6 ...... Thierry Henry (France)
        Zlatan Ibrahimović (Sweden)
        Patrick Kluivert
        (Netherlands)
        Nuno Gomes (Portugal)
        Cristiano Ronaldo (Portugal)
        Ruud van Nistelrooy
        (Netherlands)

BERTI'S DOUBLE

Berti Vogts is the only man to have won the European crown as both a player and a coach. Vogts, then with Borussia Mönchengladbach, played right-back when West Germany defeated the Soviet Union in the 1972 final in Brussels. Then he was back as a winner again 24 years later, this time as coach of the German team who beat the Czech Republic in the UEFA EURO 96 final at Wembley.

CLEAN-CUT CAPTAIN

Spain saw out the 2012 tournament conceding only one goal in their six matches. These five clean sheets kept by Spanish captain and goalkeeper Iker Casillas took his total to nine in 14 games in the finals (he had one in 2004 and three in 2008) – equalling the record held by the Netherlands' Edwin van der Sar, with his nine clean sheets from 16 matches.

ABOVE: Iker Casillas was almost unbeatable at UEFA EURO 2012, conceding one goal in six games (570 minutes). Spain's goalkeeper did not concede another goal for the next 509 minutes.

ABOVE Robert Lewandowski equalled the qualifying competition goal-scoring record with 13 as Poland qualified for UEFA EURO 2016.

LUCKY 13

Poland's Robert Lewandowski equalled the old 13-goal record of Northern Ireland's David Healy in the qualifying competition for UEFA EURO 2016. The Bayern Munich centre-forward's tally included four goals away to Gibraltar and three at home to Georgia. Healy had set his mark during qualifying for UEFA EURO 2008, and included hat-tricks against Spain and Liechtenstein.

SEEING RED

Only one man has ever been sent off in a UEFA European Football Championship final: France defender Yvon Le Roux, who received a second yellow card with five minutes remaining of his team's 2–0 triumph over Spain in 1984.

MÜLLER'S FOUR-SQUARE DEBUT

Gerd Müller netted four goals on his competitive international debut for West Germany, in a 6–0 defeat of Albania in a UEFA EURO 68 qualifier.

TOURNAMENT TOP SCORERS

1960
2 ...... François Heutte (France), Valentin Ivanov (Soviet Union), Viktor Ponedelnik (Soviet Union), Milan Galić (Yugoslavia), Dražan Jerković (Yugoslavia)

1964
2 ...... Ferenc Bene (Hungary), Dezsö Novák (Hungary), Jesús Pereda (Spain)

1968
2 ...... Dragan Džajić (Yugoslavia)

1972
4 ...... Gerd Müller (West Germany)

1976
4 ...... Dieter Müller (West Germany)

1980
3 ...... Klaus Allofs (West Germany)

1984
9 ...... Michel Platini (France)

1988
5 ...... Marco van Basten (Netherlands)

1992
3 ...... Henrik Larsen (Denmark) Karlheinz Riedle (Germany) Dennis Bergkamp (Netherlands) Tomas Brolin (Sweden)

1996
5 ...... Alan Shearer (England)

2000
5 ...... Patrick Kluivert (Netherlands) Savo Milošević (Yugoslavia)

2004
5 ...... Milan Baroš (Czech Republic)

2008
4 ...... David Villa (Spain)

2012
3 .... Mario Mandžukić (Croatia) Mario Gomez (Germany) Mario Balotelli (Italy) Cristiano Ronaldo (Portugal) Alan Dzagoev (Russia) Fernando Torres (Spain)

OTHER RECORDS

UEFA EURO FINAL REFEREES

1960	Arthur Ellis (England)
1964	Arthur Holland (England)
1968	Gottfried Dienst (Switzerland)/Replay: José Maria Ortiz De Mendibil (Spain)
1972	Ferdinand Marschall (Austria)
1976	Sergio Gonella (Italy)
1980	Nicolae Rainea (Romania)
1984	Vojtech Christov (Czechoslovakia)
1988	Michel Vautrot (France)
1992	Bruno Galler (Switzerland)
1996	Pierluigi Pairetto (Italy)
2000	Anders Frisk (Sweden)
2004	Markus Merk (Germany)
2008	Roberto Rosetti (Italy)
2012	Pedro Proença (Portugal)

KING ARTHUR

English referee Arthur Ellis took charge of the first UEFA European Nations' Cup final between the Soviet Union and Yugoslavia in 1960. Four years earlier, Ellis had also refereed the first-ever UEFA European Champion Clubs' Cup final, between Real Madrid and Reims. After he retired from football, he became the "referee" on *It's A Knockout*, the British version of the Europe-wide game show *Jeux Sans Frontières*.

SINGING IN UKRAINE

More people attended games at UEFA EURO 2012 than at any previous UEFA European Football Championship – a total of 1,440,896 across the 31 matches in Poland and Ukraine. This meant an average attendance of 46,479, the highest since 1988 (888,645 people at 15 games, for an average of 59,243). The record for most fans per match, however, is held by the five-game tournament in Italy in 1968, when an overall attendance of 299,233 meant an average of 59,847.

ENGLAND'S RECORD

The biggest official attendance at UEFA EURO 2012 was not for the final, but for a first-round Group D match, at which 64,640 fans saw England defeat Sweden 3–2, thanks to a late back-heeled winner by Danny Welbeck. In fact, the 63,170 attendance for the final was not in the top three at the finals: both the Italy v England quarter-final (64,340) and Ukraine v Sweden (64,290) in Group D attracted more spectators to the Olympic Stadium in Kyiv.

ABOVE: There were 63,170 fans in the Olympic Stadium, Kyiv, for the EURO 2012 final, but 1,470 more spectators watched England beat Sweden 3–2 there.

KEEPING IT TIGHT

UEFA EURO 2012 had the lowest goals per game average for any UEFA European Football Championship since UEFA EURO 96 in England. The 76 goals across 31 matches in Poland and Ukraine was one fewer than was scored at each of the 2004 and 2008 tournaments, and meant an average of 2.45 goals per game. It was not until the fourth of the four quarter-finals that UEFA EURO 2012 witnessed its first goalless draw, between England and Italy – but this was followed by another stalemate in the next game, three days later, between Spain and Portugal in the first of the semi-finals.

ABOVE: 69-year-old Spain coach Luis Aragones celebrates with his team after winning EURO 2008.

CO-HOST BLUES

Co-hosting has not proved a happy omen on the pitch. Belgium and the Netherlands began the trend for dual staging in 2000 followed by Austria and Switzerland in 2008 and then Poland with Ukraine in 2012. The Dutch were the only one of the six to progress beyond the group stage.

ABOVE: Joachim Löw's German teams have yet to draw in the EURO finals. He has overseen a record eight wins in a joint-record 11 matches.

REFEREE'S DOUBLE

Portuguese official Pedro Proença achieved the double feat of refereeing the 2012 UEFA Champions League final between Chelsea and Bayern Munich and that summer's UEFA EURO 2012 final between Spain and Italy. He also became the third man to referee four matches in one UEFA European Football Championship, after Sweden's Anders Frisk in 2004 and Italy's Roberto Rosetti four years later. Frisk's eight matches overall is a UEFA European Football Championship record.

RECORD HIGH FOR LÖW

Germany coach Joachim Löw claimed a record for the most UEFA European Football Championship victories in charge, when his side beat Greece 4–2 in the UEFA EURO 2012 quarter-finals. it took him to eight wins from ten games, across UEFA EURO 2008 and UEFA EURO 2012. The semi-final against Italy – while ending in defeat – also equalled compatriot Berti Vogts' record of 11 UEFA EURO finals matches as a manager.

RECORD TURN-OUTS

The record attendance for a UEFA EURO final was the 120,000 who saw Spain defeat the Soviet Union 2–1 at Real Madrid's Estadio Santiago Bernabéu on 21 June 1964. The largest crowd for any qualifying tie was the 130,711 – the overall competition record – at Hampden Park, Glasgow, on 24 February 1968 to see England draw 1–1 with Scotland. It saw England reach the quarter-finals at the Scots' expense.

NAME GAME

Players wore their names as well as their numbers on the back of their shirts for the first time at UEFA EURO 1992. They had previously been identified by numbers only.

WINNING AGE

Luis Aragonés is the oldest coach of the European champions. Aragonés (born in Madrid on 28 July 1938) was 29 days short of his 70th birthday when Spain beat Germany 1–0 in the UEFA EURO 2008 final in Vienna.

UEFA EURO 2016
Match Schedule

EURO2016
FRANCE

Fill in the results as the tournament unfolds and find out if your fancied teams for the finals live up to your expectations.

GROUP A

Match	Date	Time	Venue	Fixture	Score
1	Fri 10 June	20:00	Stade de France	France vs Romania	☐ - ☐
2	Sat 11 June	14:00	Lens	Albania vs Switz	☐ - ☐
14	Wed 15 June	17:00	Parc des Princes	Romania vs Switz	☐ - ☐
15	Wed 15 June	20:00	Marseille	France vs Albania	☐ - ☐
25	Sun 19 June	20:00	Lyon	Romania vs Albania	☐ - ☐
26	Sun 19 June	20:00	Lille	Switz vs France	☐ - ☐

GROUP A Final Table

Team	P	W	D	L	F	A	GD	Pts
1								
2								
3								
4								

GROUP B

Match	Date	Time	Venue	Fixture	Score
3	Sat 11 June	17:00	Bordeaux	Wales vs Slovakia	☐ - ☐
4	Sat 11 June	20:00	Marseille	England vs Russia	☐ - ☐
13	Wed 15 June	14:00	Lille	Russia vs Slovakia	☐ - ☐
16	Thu 16 June	14:00	Lens	England vs Wales	☐ - ☐
27	Mon 20 June	20:00	Toulouse	Russia vs Wales	☐ - ☐
28	Mon 20 June	20:00	St-Étienne	Slovakia vs England	☐ - ☐

GROUP B Final Table

Team	P	W	D	L	F	A	GD	Pts
1								
2								
3								
4								

GROUP C

Match	Date	Time	Venue	Fixture	Score
6	Sun 12 June	17:00	Nice	Poland vs N. Ireland	☐ - ☐
7	Sun 12 June	20:00	Lille	Germany vs Ukraine	☐ - ☐
17	Thu 16 June	17:00	Lyon	Ukraine vs N. Ireland	☐ - ☐
18	Thu 16 June	20:00	Stade de France	Germany vs Poland	☐ - ☐
29	Tue 21 June	17:00	Marseille	Ukraine vs Poland	☐ - ☐
30	Tue 21 June	17:00	Parc des Princes	N. Ire vs Germany	☐ - ☐

GROUP C Final Table

Team	P	W	D	L	F	A	GD	Pts
1								
2								
3								
4								

GROUP D

Match	Date	Time	Venue	Fixture	Score
5	Sun 12 June	14:00	Parc des Princes	Turkey vs Croatia	☐ - ☐
8	Mon 13 June	14:00	Toulouse	Spain vs Czech Rep	☐ - ☐
20	Fri 17 June	17:00	St-Étienne	Czech Rep vs Croatia	☐ - ☐
21	Fri 17 June	20:00	Nice	Spain vs Turkey	☐ - ☐
31	Tue 21 June	20:00	Lens	Czech Rep vs Turkey	☐ - ☐
32	Tue 21 June	20:00	Bordeaux	Croatia vs Spain	☐ - ☐

GROUP D Final Table

Team	P	W	D	L	F	A	GD	Pts
1								
2								
3								
4								

GROUP E

Match	Date	Time	Venue	Fixture	Score
9	Mon 13 June	17:00	Stade de France	Rep Ire vs Sweden	☐-☐
10	Mon 13 June	20:00	Lyon	Belgium vs Italy	☐-☐
19	Fri 17 June	14:00	Toulouse	Italy vs Sweden	☐-☐
22	Sat 18 June	14:00	Bordeaux	Belgium vs Rep Ire	☐-☐
35	Wed 22 June	20:00	Lille	Italy vs Rep Ireland	☐-☐
36	Wed 22 June	20:00	Nice	Sweden vs Belgium	☐-☐

GROUP E Final Table

Team	P	W	D	L	F	A	GD	Pts
1								
2								
3								
4								

GROUP F

Match	Date	Time	Venue	Fixture	Score
11	Tue 14 June	17:00	Bordeaux	Austria vs Hungary	☐-☐
12	Tue 14 June	20:00	St-Étienne	Portugal vs Iceland	☐-☐
23	Sat 18 June	17:00	Marseille	Iceland vs Hungary	☐-☐
24	Sat 18 June	20:00	Parc des Princes	Portugal vs Austria	☐-☐
33	Wed 22 June	17:00	Stade de France	Iceland vs Austria	☐-☐
34	Wed 22 June	17:00	Lyon	Hungary vs Portugal	☐-☐

GROUP F Final Table

Team	P	W	D	L	F	A	GD	Pts
1								
2								
3								
4								

LAST 16

Match	Date	Time	Venue	Fixture	Score
L1	Sat 25 June	14:00	St-Étienne	A2 vs C2	☐-☐
L2	Sat 25 June	17:00	Parc des Princes	B1 vs ACD3	☐-☐
L3	Sat 25 June	20:00	Lens	D1 vs BEF3	☐-☐
L4	Sun 26 June	14:00	Lyon	A1 vs CDE3	☐-☐
L5	Sun 26 June	17:00	Lille	C1 vs ABF3	☐-☐
L6	Sun 26 June	20:00	Toulouse	F1 vs E2	☐-☐
L7	Mon 27 June	17:00	Stade de France	E1 vs D2	☐-☐
L8	Mon 27 June	20:00	Nice	B2 vs F2	☐-☐

Quarter-Finals

Match	Date	Time	Venue	Fixture	Score
Q1	Thu 30 June	20:00	Marseille	L1 vs L3	☐-☐
Q2	Fri 1 July	20:00	Lille	L2 vs L6	☐-☐
Q3	Sat 2 July	20:00	Bordeaux	L5 vs L7	☐-☐
Q4	Sun 3 July	20:00	Stade de France	L4 vs L8	☐-☐

SEMI-FINALS

S1 ✪ Wed 5 July ✪ 20:00 ✪ Lyon

Q1	vs	Q2

S2 ✪ Thu 6 July ✪ 20:00 ✪ Marseille

Q3	vs	Q4

FINAL

Sun 10 July ✪ 20:00 ✪ Stade de France

S1	vs	S2

NOTE: These kick-off times are British Summer Time (BST), one hour behind CET, the local time in France.

PICTURE CREDITS

ABOVE: Super Victor, the UEFA EURO 2016 mascot, indicates at the finals draw that France intends the entire tournament to be a winner.

The publishers would like to thank the following sources for their kind permission to reproduce the pictures in this book. (T-top, C-centre, B-bottom, L-left, R-right)

Colorsport: 106; /Andrew Cowie: 111; / Mike Wall: 105. **Getty Images:** /AFP: 108; / Allsport: 19TR, 118-119; /Gonzalo Arroyo Moreno: 70BL; /Lars Baron/Bongarts: 84BL, 114; /Shaun Botterill: 32-33, 98-99, 110, 120, 121BL; /Paulo Bruno: 35; /Giuseppe Cacace/ AFP: 76BR; /Central Press/Hulton Archive: 103; /Michal Cizek/AFP: 73; /Fabrice Coffrini/ AFP: 46BR; /Patricia de Melo Moreira/AFP: 7BC; /Philippe Desmazes/AFP: 12; /Matej Divizna: 72BR; /Denis Doyle: 78-79, 125TR; / Tom Dulat: 92BL, 93; /Emmanuel Dunand/ AFP: 80BL; /Yurko Dyachyshyn/AFP: 64BL; / Epsilon: 56BL, 56BR, 76BL; /Franck Fife/AFP: 13, 16, 40BL, 40BR; /Stu Forster: 6BL, 6BCL, 27, 52BR, 53; /Louisa Gouliamaki/AFP: 31; / Laurence Griffiths: 6BCR, 22, 30, 38-39, 47, 50BR, 51, 91; /Alex Grimm: 100-101; /Dennis Grombkowski/Bongarts: 7BR, 85; /Jack Guez/ AFP: 20-21; /Valery Hache/AFP: 17; /Matthias Hangst: 9; /Matthias Hangst/Bongarts: 29; / Alexander Hassenstein/Bongarts: 60BL, 84BR; /Mike Hewitt: 6BR, 70BR; /Christian Hofer: 94BL, 95; /Horstmüller/ullstein bild: 109; / Boris Horvat/AFP: 15, 122; /Karim Jaafar/ AFP: 74BL; /Keystone: 18; /Attila Kisbenedek/ AFP: 96BL, 96BR, 97; /Joe Klamar/AFP: 55; / Halldor Kolbeins/AFP: 92BR; /Ozan Kose/ AFP: 72BL, 75; /Samuel Kubani/AFP: 50BL, 54BR, 94BR; /Kirill Kudryavtsev/AFP: 34; / Pascal Le Segetain: 8; /Christopher Lee: 115; /Mark Leech: 68-69; /Alex Livesey: 24-25; / Marco Luzzani: 77; /Ian MacNicol: 7BL, 63; /Jure Makovec/AFP: 65; /Cesar Manso/ AFP: 28; /Jamie McDonald: 121TR; /Charles McQuillan: 37, 66BR, 67; /Miguel Medina/ AFP: 60BR; /Daniel Mihailescu/AFP: 42BL; / Filippo Monteforte/AFP: 123BL; /Jonathan Nackstrand/AFP: 86BR; /Adam Nurkiewicz: 123TC; /Valerio Pennicino: 42BR, 43; /Stephen Pond: 66BL, 86BL; /Popperfoto: 19BL, 112; / Adam Pretty/Bongarts: 61; /Tullio M Puglia: 82BR; /Ben Radford: 116-117; /David Ramos: 88-89; /Miguel Riopa/AFP: 45, 90BR; /Martin Rose: 87, 124; /STR/AFP: 74BR; /Philipp Schmidli: 46BL; / Juan Manuel Serrano Arce: 71; /Gent Shkullaku/AFP: 36, 44BL, 48-49; /Janek Skarzynski/AFP: 62BL; /Anatolii Stepanov/AFP: 64BR; /Srdjan Stevanovic: 41, 52BL, 58-59; /Patrik Stollarz/AFP: 125BL; / Sergei Supinsky/AFP: 54BL; /Bob Thomas: 107, 113; /John Thys/AFP: 80BR, 90BL; /VI-Images: 26; /Loic Venance/AFP: 23, 44BR, 128; /Claudio Villa: 81, 82BL, 83; /Ian Walton: 62BR. **Offside Sports Photography:** /L'Equipe: 102, 104. **PA Images:** /Thibault Camus/AP: 4-5; /Michel Euler/AP: 10-11; /Ivan Sekretarev/AP: 57

Every effort has been made to acknowledge correctly and contact the source and/or copyright holder of each picture and Carlton Books Limited apologizes for any unintentional errors or omissions that will be corrected in future editions of this book.